MathTivities!

Classroom Activities for Grades 1-6

 Creative Publications®

Wadsworth Publishing Company

I(T)P® An International Thomson Publishing Company

Belmont, CA• Albany, NY • Bonn • Boston • Cincinnati • Detroit • Johannesburg • London • Madrid •
Melbourne • Mexico City• New York • Paris • Singapore • Tokyo • Toronto • Washington

Education Editor: Sabra Horne
Assistant Editor: Claire Masson
Editorial Assistant: Kate Barrett
Marketing Manager: Mike Dew
Senior Production Editor: Debby Kramer
Production: Robin Gold/Forbes Mill Press
Print Buyer: Karen Hunt
Permissions Editor: Jeanne Bosschart
Cover Designer: Randall Goodall/Seventeenth Street Studios
Printer: Globus Printing Co.

Printed in the United States of America
1 2 3 4 5 6 7 8 9 10—01 00 99 98 97 96 95

For more information, contact Wadsworth Publishing Company:

International Thomson Publishing Europe
Berkshire House 168-173
High Holborn
London, WC1V 7AA, England

International Thomson Editores
Campos Eliseos 385, Piso 7
Col. Polanco
11560 México D.F. México

Thomas Nelson Australia
102 Dodds Street
South Melbourne 3205
Victoria, Australia

International Thomson Publishing Asia
221 Henderson Road
#05-10 Henderson Building
Singapore 0315

Thomas Nelson Canada
1120 Birchmount Road
Scarborough, Ontario
Canada M1K 5G4

International Thomson Publishing Japan
Hirakawacho Kyowa Building, 3F
2-2-1 Hirakawacho
Chiyoda-ku, Tokyo 102, Japan

International Thomson Publishing GmbH
Königswinterer Strasse 418
53227 Bonn, Germany

International Thomson Publishing Southern Africa
Building 18, Constantia Park
240 Old Pretoria Road
Halfway House, 1685 South Africa

ISBN 0-534-52740-X

Contents

Notes to the User of
MathTivities!: Classroom Activities for Grades 1–6

What is MathTivities!?

MathTivities! Classroom Activities for Grades 1–6 is a supplemental book for Kennedy-Tipps, (1997), *Guiding Children Learning of Mathematics*, 8th Edition (Wadsworth Publishing Company), that contains selected activities from six series of publications produced by Creative Publications: *Connections, Constructing Ideas, Linking Math and Technology, Mathematical Pathways Through Literature, 20 Thinking Questions*, and *Writing Mathematics*.

    MathTivities! contains 48 activities for grades 1–6. The teacher-directed activities are designed to help children understand concepts and processes. The activities emphasize the use of technology and manipulative materials, problem solving, group processes, discussion and writing, and thinking and applications. The activities deal with problem solving, reasoning, communication, and connections, discussed in Chapter 1 of *Guiding Children's Learning of Mathematics*, and the mathematics topics discussed in Part 2 of the book.

    In its *Curriculum and Evaluation Standards for School Mathematics*, published in 1989, the National Council of Teachers of Mathematics (NCTM) stressed that mathematics is problem solving and that all students should learn to reason and communicate about mathematics and make connections within mathematics and between mathematics and the world in which they live. Activities in *MathTivities!* were selected because they exemplify the types of activities that enable children to construct meanings in and develop conceptual understandings of mathematics.

    Books in the Creative Publications sets from which selections were made for *MathTivities!* can be divided into two classes: Three of the sets—*Connections, Constructing Ideas*, and *20 Thinking Questions*—feature activities with manipulatives that help students develop an understanding of concepts and processes. In the other sets, each lesson develops an important mathematical idea, with a special emphases for each book: *Linking Math and Technology* has activities for which a computer is an integral part. *Mathematical Pathways*

Through Literature suggests ways to use children's literature to promote understanding of mathematics. The emphasis in *Writing Mathematics* is on students using oral and written language as tools for learning and understanding mathematics.

The Philosophy of MathTivities!

The philosophy of *MathTivities!* parallels that of *Guiding Children's Learning of Mathematics*, 8th Edition by Leonard Kennedy and Steve Tipps, who believe that students learn mathematics best when they develop their own understandings of concepts and processes. Teachers serve as instigators and facilitators of learning who guide children's thinking in a variety of ways and with a variety of materials. Lessons selected for *MathTivities!* reflect this belief.

    The 48 activity-based lessons cover all major mathematics topics that are part of the elementary school curriculum: numbers and numeration, common and decimal fractions, computation, measurement, statistics and data analysis, patterns, geometry, sorting and classifying, money, probability, and estimation. The activities are designed to encourage student thinking about and facilitate their understanding of mathematics. Manipulative materials are involved in nearly all. Some lessons present topics that are new to children and can be used to introduce a new concept or process. Others extend student's understanding of already known topics. Each lesson is teacher directed, and all activities involve students in problem solving and reasoning, as well as oral and written communication.

Classroom Practices That Promote Effective Learning

The goals of the NCTM and state and local education agencies will not be accomplished in classrooms in which a teacher and a textbook dominate learning and teaching practices emphasize numbers and computation and rely on rote learning and memorization.

Practices that promote conceptual understanding rely on a variety of materials, resources, and teacher-student behaviors. The emphases are on helping students make sense of numbers and processes; use calculators, paper and pencil, and mental arithmetic to compute; deal with geometry and measurement as related topics; learn about patterns, statistics, and probability; develop spatial visualization skills; and engage in meaningful problem solving. The teacher's role is not to impart knowledge but, rather, to guide children's learning of mathematics.

The following teacher practices are compatible with the lessons in *MathTivities!* and will help empower students in mathematics:

- The teacher provides a relaxed atmosphere for learning.
- The teacher uses a variety of procedures and materials to help students make sense of mathematics and avoids the "open-your-book-and-follow-along-as-I-explain" routine.
- The teacher facilitates learning by creating situations that allow children to learn concepts and processes individually, in small groups, and through whole-class activities.
- The teacher guides interactions by using probing and open-ended questions. At times a teacher is quiet and listens to what children say.
- The teacher values processes and thinking as well as answers. Students' processes and thinking are acknowledged and credited even when a solution is incomplete or only partially correct.
- The teacher engages in ongoing assessment of both students and her or his teaching practices.
- The teacher balances all aspects of mathematics. Work with numbers and computation is important and included, but does not dominate the program to the exclusion of other topics.
- The teacher respects students' feelings. Humiliation, sarcasm, and ridicule are not used by the teacher or students. Students' errors and misconceptions are usually the result of incomplete understanding of a concept or process and are used as a basis for further teaching and clarification of concepts and processes.

Just as the role of a teacher has changed, so has that of a student. Each student assumes greater responsibility for her or his learning. These student behaviors are encouraged by lessons in this book:

- The student is an active participant in the process of learning mathematics.
- The student works in a variety of settings: independent, small-group, and whole-class.
- The student uses a variety of concrete, pictorial, graphic and symbolic and electronic materials to model concepts and complete procedures.
- The student engages in small-group and whole-class discussions to clarify thinking. Understanding develops as concrete and other models are linked to written and verbal symbols.
- The student writes about mathematics to clarify her or his thinking and to explain concepts and processes. Writing is done as problems are solved and to organize and explain data, compute answers, and report results of work done.
- The student uses concepts and processes in meaningful contexts. Applications of mathematics provide motivation for learning and make connections to the real world

The Creative Publications Series in MathTivities!

Connections

Connections is a series of eight resource books for grades 1 to 8. Each book contains 20 manipulative lessons designed to teach the most important mathematics topics for its grade. The series is based on the philosophy that active learning with manipulative materials is the foundation upon which children build their understanding of mathematics. Students explore with manipulatives; discuss, record, and organize their findings; then display and report what they have found. Typically, lessons involve children working in one of three groupings:

- Eight groups of four, sharing materials, working together
- Eight groups of four, sharing materials, working independently
- Eight groups of four, sharing materials, working in pairs

Sometimes six groups of five or five groups of six are used. The class occasionally works as a whole.

Each lesson is divided into four parts. The first page gives the title, manipulative, mathematics topic, a short description of the lesson, the recommended grouping plan, and a materials list. The second page contains directions for the lesson, including ideas for beginning and a step-by-step plan using materials to explore the concept, as well as recommendations for recording students' findings. Ways to involve students in reporting, discussing, and organizing their findings, along with typical student work are on the third page. The final page(s) has a student recording sheet master page for the activity.

Constructing Ideas

Constructing Ideas is a set of nine books, three each for grades 1–3, 3–4, and 5–6. Each book features a major theme: counting, number combinations, and patterns in the first set; multiplication and division, large numbers, and common fractions in the second set; and data analysis, fractional numbers, and geometry in the third set. Each book is based on the belief that students learn best when they think, invent, and make connections; ask questions and set up challenges; and observe, question, and listen. Student thinking and reasoning are heavily emphasized.

A lesson consists of a topic for exploration, reproducible homework pages, and teacher resource pages. The first page identifies the exploration and concepts students will investigate, lists materials, and explains preparatory steps. The second page includes a complete set of instructions, including ideas of what might be said to students helpful advice and hints, and a summary of the homework assignment. Page three contains instructions for student investigations that can be duplicated to guide children working in pairs or small groups (occasionally, students work independently or as a whole class). Suggested questions are provided to encourage student thought and demonstrate understanding. Questions to foster reflection after an investigation is completed are included. The final page(s) contains examples of student work to give the teacher an idea of what students might do. Each lesson has a homework page.

Linking Math and Technology

Linking Math and Technology is a set of 7 books, one for each grade K–6. Each book contains 10 lessons designed to give in-depth investigations during which students produce original reports and projects, organize materials, give solutions that reflect personal understandings, use manipulatives, and work in small groups. The lessons augment any curriculum by providing examples of ways to link computer use to an ongoing program. Lessons can continue over any number of days, depending on available equipment. The lessons are keyed to The Cruncher and The Multimedia Workshop (both by Davidson and Associates) computer programs, available for Macintosh or Windows and in English and Spanish. They can be done with other comparable programs.

Each lesson has the same components. A statement about the nature of each investigation, list of materials, ways to trigger student thinking and get them started, step-by-step computer directions, and culminating activities are presented for each lesson.

Mathematical Pathways Through Literature

This series has a book for each grade 1–6. Twelve mathematics lessons are followed by two extension activities based on a children's book. Fiction and nonfiction books have selected for their ability to extend the mathematical concept presented in a lesson. Lessons involve students in an investigation and encourage inquiry and appreciation of literature. The books involve students emotionally, provide an extension of a mathematics idea to open the way for further inquiry, and provide visuals that help clarify ideas and concepts.

The guide for each lesson has a one-page investigation plan, including a list of materials and explanation of the preparation needed for the lesson. A literature summary page identifies a book, gives a synopsis, and offers suggestions for using the book. Each of the other pages contains an extension of the lesson based on the book.

20 Thinking Questions

20 Thinking Questions is a series of 10 books for grades 1–3 and 3–6. Each book encourages development of mathematical understanding through activities with a specific manipulative material. Materials involved in lessons in **MathTivities!** are Sorting Treasures, Pattern Blocks, Base 10 Blocks, and Rainbow Cubes, all available from Creative Publications. Activities are based on the philosophy that students must explore mathematics concepts with manipulative materials and have opportunities to think and write about what they are doing. Activities can be used to augment an existing curriculum when it is appropriate to instigate student thinking and writing about specific concepts.

Each lesson has a common format. The question being asked and a list of materials are on the first page. "Introducing the Lesson" describes how a teacher can introduce a whole-class activity. Suggestions of what to do depending on students approaches to problems follow the introduction. Examples of student solutions show how students might respond. Assessment is covered in "What to Look For in Student's Work." Following class discussion, students are given time to reflect on their work by making entries in their journals. "Journal Reflection" questions guide this work.

Writing Mathematics

The resource book for each grades 1–6 in this series emphasize writing about mathematics. Each book contains 10 lessons that encourage students to develop oral and written language as tools for learning and communicating mathematical ideas. Lessons involve students in both informal and structured expository writing.

The same lesson format used is used in this series: a lesson overview, plans for a mathematics investigation and a writing extension, assessment criteria, and ideas for promoting discourse for each lesson. The assessment criteria focus on stu-dents' thinking about concepts and on the writing process and formats. The questions can be used for writing scoring rubrics for each lesson. Students have opportunities for self-assessment as they reflect on their writing and discuss it with class-mates.

Manipulatives Needed for Lessons

The manipulatives used with *MathTivities!* are commonly found in many classrooms. All materials can be purchased from Creative Publications. In some instances, teacher-gathered materials can be used in place of a specified manipulative. These manipulative materials are featured in lessons in this book:

- Pattern Blocks, for students and overhead projector
- Rainbow Cubes
- Base 10 Blocks, for students and overhead projector
- Plastic Coins
- Teddy Bear Counters, for students and overhead projector
- Sorting Treasures
- Tangrams, for students and overhead projector
- Geoboards

A Guide to MathTivities!

Connections

Grade	Activity Title	Pages	Kennedy Chapter	Description
One	Measure Me	2–5	12	Measurement Patterns
One	Crazy Quilts	6–9	1 and 9	Patterns
Two	Picturing Addition	10–13	7	Addition
Two	Tiny Turtle Parade	14–17	1 and 9	Patterns/Problem Solving
Three	1000 Count	18–21	6	Base 10 and Counting
Three	Tangramarea	22–25	9 and 12	Geometry/Area
Four	Pentomino Challenge	26–29	9	Pattern
Four	Magic Decimal Point	30–34	10	Base 10 & Decimals
Five	Rare Rectangles	35–38	1 and 9	Geometry and Patterns
Five	Rainbow Square Cubes	39–43	1 & 6	Patterns and Problem Solving
Six	Rainbow and Factors	44–47	6 & 11	Cubes and Factors
Six	Make a Million	48–51	6	Base 10 and Large Numbers

20 Thinking Questions

Book Title	Grade	Activity Title	Pages	Kennedy Chapter	Description
Sorting Treasures	One	How Can You Sort Treasures?	54–57	5	Classifying and Sorting
Sorting Treasures	One	How Are the Buttons Alike and Different?	58–61	5	Sorting/Differences

Connections

Measure Me

In this lesson, children use Unifix Cubes to measure different parts of their bodies (length of arm, smile, and so on). The activity gives them a hands-on experience with nonstandard measurement. Use during your chapter on measurement.

Classroom Organization

Eight groups of four sharing materials
Working together

Materials

Each group of four children:
• 75 Unifix® Cubes in random colors • 4 copies of Measure Me Recording Sheet, page 5 • 4 four-foot sheets of butcher paper • Scissors, crayons and paste

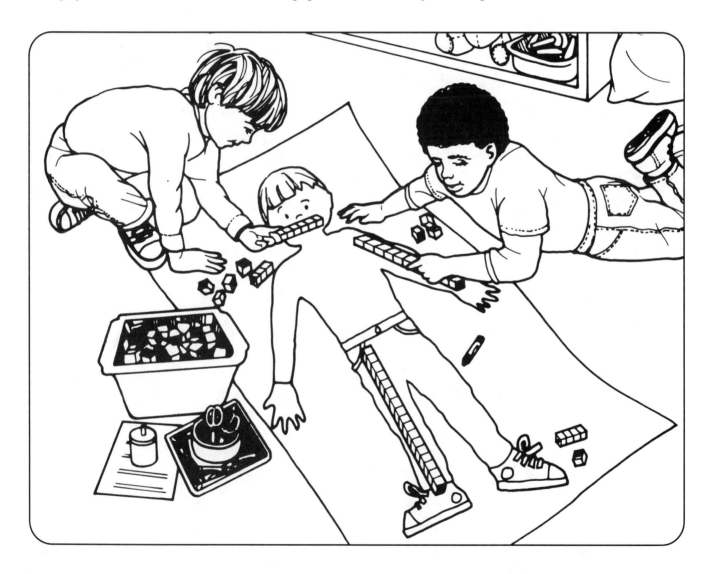

Introducing the Problem

How tall do you think you are? How long is your nose? How wide is your smile? Today we are going to measure and find out.

How many Unifix Cubes do you think it will take to measure the length of your hand?

Exploring with Unifix® Cubes

1. Tell the children to make a stick of Unifix Cubes that is just as long as their hand from the wrist to the tip of their longest finger. Let them compare the different sticks within their group.

2. Challenge the children to find out how tall they are in terms of cubes. Have them work together in pairs to draw outlines of one another on the pieces of butcher paper.

Recording the Connection

1. Tell the children to measure their heights using Unifix Cubes and record their findings on their recording sheets.

2. Have them continue using Unifix Cubes to measure the lengths of their noses, arms, legs, feet, and other body parts, then record the information on their recording sheets.

3. Then have the children color their body prints and label them with the tags from their recording sheets.

Reporting and Displaying

When all the body prints are completed, discuss and compare them. Ask the children what they found out from their measuring. Discuss different ways to display the prints on a wall or bulletin board. Choose one of the ways children suggest.

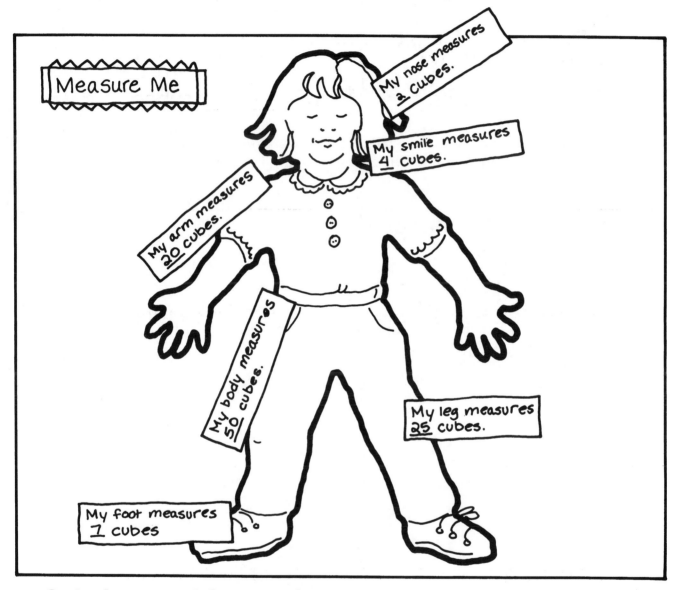

Solutions and Suggestions

There are many different ways to organize the body prints for an interesting display. They could be put in order from tallest to shortest. They could be sorted based on width of smile, length of arm, length of leg, and so on. Give the children many opportunities to discuss the likenesses and differences among the prints.

Measure Me

My nose measures
_____ cubes.

My leg measures
_____ cubes.

My arm measures
_____ cubes.

My foot measures
_____ cubes.

My body measures
_____ cubes.

My smile measures
_____ cubes.

Measure Me Recording Sheet

Crazy Quilts

In this lesson, children try to build hexagons with different numbers of Pattern Blocks and then use the designs or make an interesting geometric pattern. Use in conjunction with your textbook chapter on geometry.

Classroom Organization

Eight groups of four sharing materials
Working together

Materials

Each group of four children will need these following materials:
• Pattern Blocks • 4 copies of Crazy Quilts Recording Sheet, page 9 •1 sheet of 12" × 18" black construction paper • Scissors, Crayons, and paste

Introducing the Problem

Today, each group is going to make a crazy quilt using pieces shaped like this (Show the yellow hexagon block.) There are nine different ways to cover the shape with Pattern Blocks.

Can you find some ways?

Exploring with Pattern Blocks

1. Tell the groups to try making the hexagon with different combinations of Pattern Blocks.

2. Tell the group to keep working until everyone has found several different ways to make the hexagon.

3. Tell the group to decide on one design they like best. They should color the design nine times on their recording sheets.

4. Then have them cut out their hexagons. Each group should have 36 pieces.

Recording the Connection

1. Give each group a piece of 12" x 18" black construction paper. Have each group arrange their 36 hexagons on the black paper to make a crazy quilt.

2. When they are satisfied with their design, have them paste the pieces down.

Reporting and Displaying

Display the finished pieces on a crazy quilt bulletin board. Compare the designs and discuss the different patterns the groups have made their hexagons.

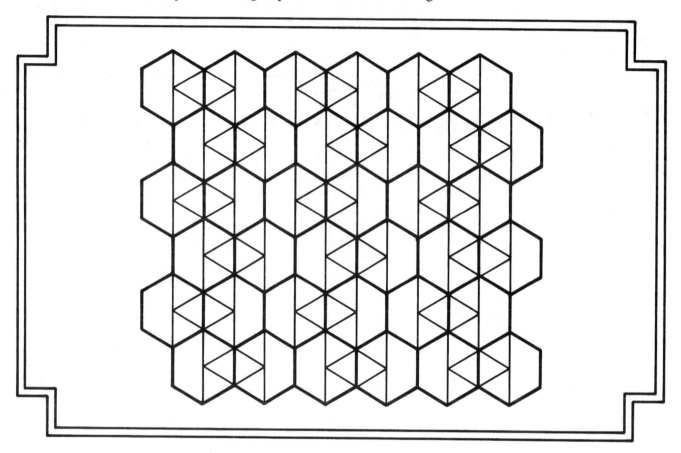

Solutions and Suggestions

There are nine different ways to fill the hexagon shape. There are many different ways to make a crazy quilt.

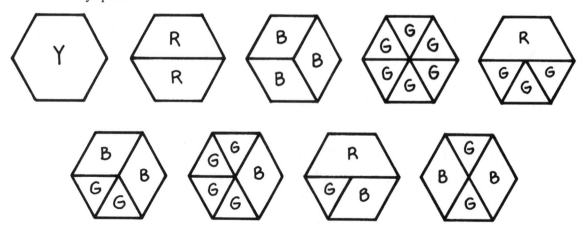

Crazy Quilts

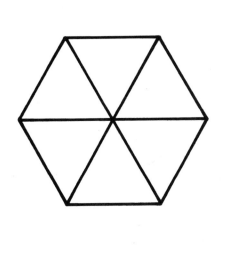 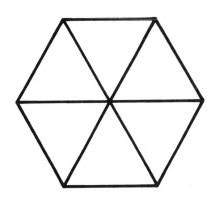 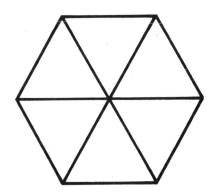

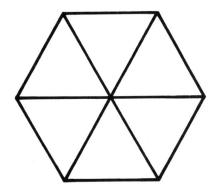 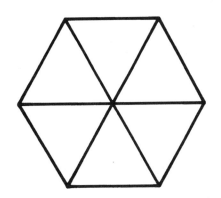 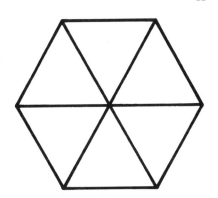

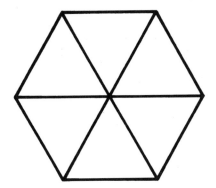 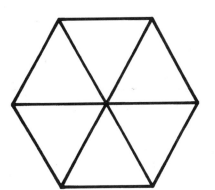 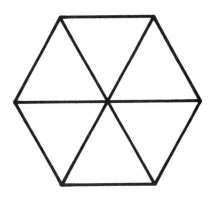

Crazy Quilts Recording Sheet

Picturing Addition

In this lesson, children learn to apply regrouping skills to two-digit addition problems. They use cubes to represent problems and they link the addition algorithm to the way the cubes look. Use after children have had experience with regrouping and are starting to use the addition algorithm.

Classroom Organization

Eight groups of four sharing materials
Working together

Materials

Each group of four children will need these materials:
• 75 Unifix® Cubes • 8 copies of Picturing Addition Recording Sheet, page 13

Introducing the Problem

Today you are going to work together and use your cubes to make pictures of addition problems.

What do you think a picture of an addition problem looks like?

Exploring with Unifix® Cubes

1. Write this problem and it's solution on the chalkboard. Challenge the children to work together in their groups and show the problem with cubes. Have them show a way to find the answer with those cubes.

$$\begin{array}{r} 36 \\ + 16 \\ \hline 52 \end{array}$$

2. When everyone has made an attempt, give different children an opportunity to describe what they did. They have some version of 3 tens, 6 ones in one place and 1 ten, 6 ones in another place. After they move the cubes to add, they should have 5 tens and 2 ones. Have them tell what they did to get the answer.

3. Erase the answer and tell the children to watch as you solve the problem *the math way* writing down the 2, carrying the 1, and writing the 5. Have the children look at their cubes and *the math way* of finding the answer to the problem. Ask them why they think we write the numbers like this.

   - Can you see the 12 ones in the cubes ? In the problem?
   - Can you see the 4 tens in the cubes? In the problem?
   - Can you see the regrouped ones (the new ten)? In the cubes? In the problem?
   - Why do you think we write *2* and put a *1* above the problem?

Recording the Connection

1. Have the children work together to make up and solve their own addition problems with Unifix Cubes.

2. Show them how to record their work on the Picturing Addition Recording Sheet (page 12). Encourage them to do several different problems.

Reporting and Displaying

After the groups have completed several different recording sheets, discuss a few of them together. It is important for children to have many opportunities to explain how the numbers in the problems relate to the way the cubes look. The goal is for children to be able to picture their addition problems with cubes and then explain how the numbers work.

Children may wish to put their recording sheets together into booklets. Unifix Cubes and extra recording sheets could also be set up as an independent math center where children could continue working on addition problems on another day.

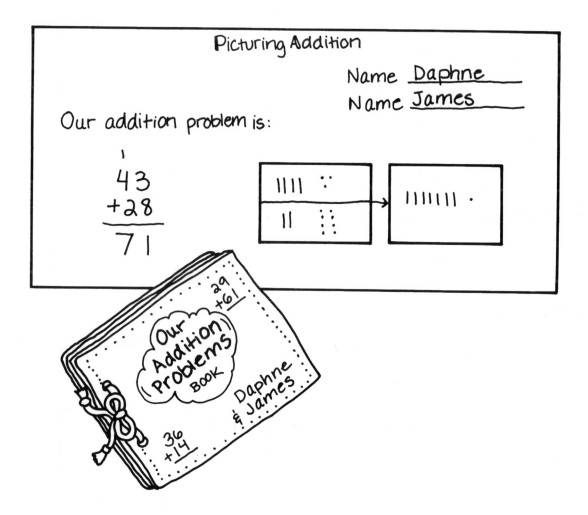

Suggestions

For more activity ideas, see *Understanding Place Value: Addition and Subtraction,* Creative Publications, Catalog Number 10965.

Picturing Addition

Names _____

_____

Our addition problem is:

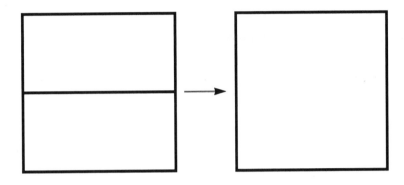

- -

Picturing Addition

Names _____

_____

Our addition problem is:

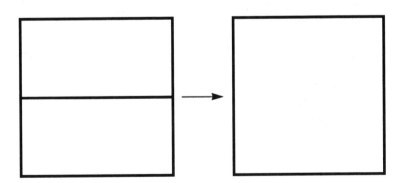

Tiny Turtle Parade

In this lesson, children use Pattern Blocks to cover a turtle outline. They exchange blocks for other blocks to find different ways to cover the same ways space. Use this lesson to enhance visual thinking, spatial skills, and problem-solving abilities.

Classroom Organization

Eight groups of four sharing materials
Working together

Materials

Each group of four children will need these materials:
Pattern Blocks • 4 copies of Tiny Turtle Parade Recording Sheet, page 17 • Crayons

Introducing the Problem

The tiny turtles are going out to march in the parade. They always march in order with the turtles covered with the least number of blocks at the front of the line.

How many different turtles do you think will march in the parade?

Exploring with Pattern Blocks

1. Tell the children to cover the turtles on their recording sheets with blocks. Note that there is a triangle grid inside the turtle to help the children when they color to record. Blocks other than triangles will fit on the grid, and children should be encouraged to use them to cover the turtle.

2. Have children count the number of blocks they used.

3. Explain to the groups that their task is to find four different ways to cover the turtle with blocks.

Recording the Connection

1. When the groups have found four different ways to cover the turtle, they should record each way by coloring the grids to show the blocks.

2. Below the turtles, they should write the number of blocks used in each solution.

Reporting and Displaying

When each group has four turtles covered with different numbers of blocks, work together as a class to make the parade. Find the turtles covered with the least number of blocks, the next greater, and so on to the turtles covered with the greatest number of blocks.

Some groups may want to use extra recording sheets to find ways with other numbers of blocks.

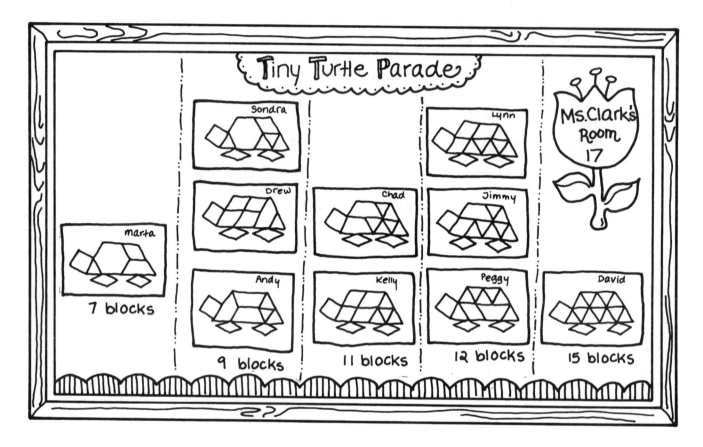

Solutions and Suggestions

The least number of blocks needed to cover the Tiny Turtle is 7. The greatest number of blocks needed is 15. It is possible to cover Tiny Turtle with every number of blocks in between.

For more activity ideas, see *Hands on Pattern Blocks,* Creative Publications, Catalog Number 34489

Tiny Turtle Parade

Name ______________________

Number of blocks ________

Tiny Turtle Parade Recording Sheet

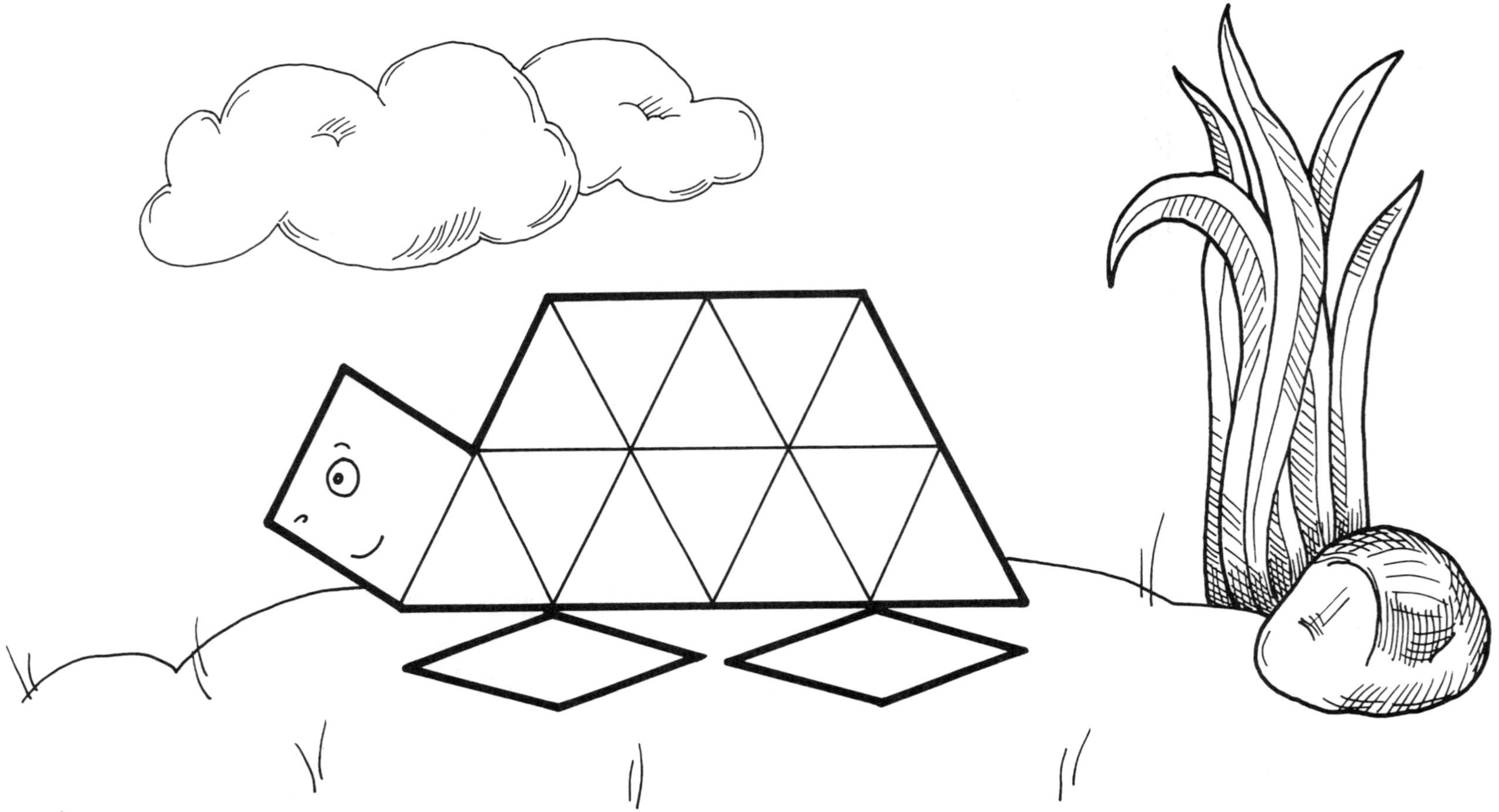

1000 Count

In this lesson, students group base ten blocks together into hundreds, putting them into grid paper jackets. They count the blocks by hundreds recording by writing the numbers. The whole class together will count to 2800. Use this lesson to introduce the concept of thousands and to build an understanding of larger numbers.

Classroom Organization

Five groups of six sharing materials
Working together

Materials

• Base Ten Blocks: 2 hundreds-blocks, 30 ten-blocks, 60 ones-blocks • 6 copies of 1000 Count Recording Sheet, page 21 • Scissors and tape • Strip of paper long enough to write the numbers 100–2800 by hundreds

Introducing the Problem

Today we are going to count all the Base Ten Blocks we have out on our tables. We are going to group them together into hundreds to make it easier to count them.

What number do you think tells the total value of the Base Ten Blocks?

Exploring with Base Ten Blocks

1. Tell the students to work together to make as many groups of 100 as they can with their blocks.

2. Show them how to make a hundreds-jacket by cutting out the pattern on the recording sheet, folding up the sides, and taping the corners.

3. Have them work together to make six jackets and fill them with the Base Ten Blocks (five jackets will be filled, one will have 60 in it).

4. Have the class combine the hundreds on the table. Let one student at a time bring a filled jacket to the table. Count together by hundreds, with someone writing the numbers on the long strip of paper as each hundreds-jacket is added to the group. When there are ten hundreds-jackets, stack them up to make 1000. When all the completely-filled jackets have been used, students from two groups should combine blocks to make more hundreds-jackets.

5. Stop at random points and discuss the relationship between the way the blocks look and the number that is being written.

6. Continue until all the blocks have been used. You should reach the number 2800.

Recording the Connection

1. After the counting is completed, remove the blocks from the jackets.

2. Have students write the numbers inside the empty jackets, skip-counting from 100 to 2800

Reporting and Displaying

Arrange the empty hundreds-jackets so students can see the skip-counting numbers. Later, mix up the jackets and give them to a small group of students to rearrange in order.

Some students may want to make more jackets and extend the numbers. How far would you get if you put hundreds-jackets a line all around the room?

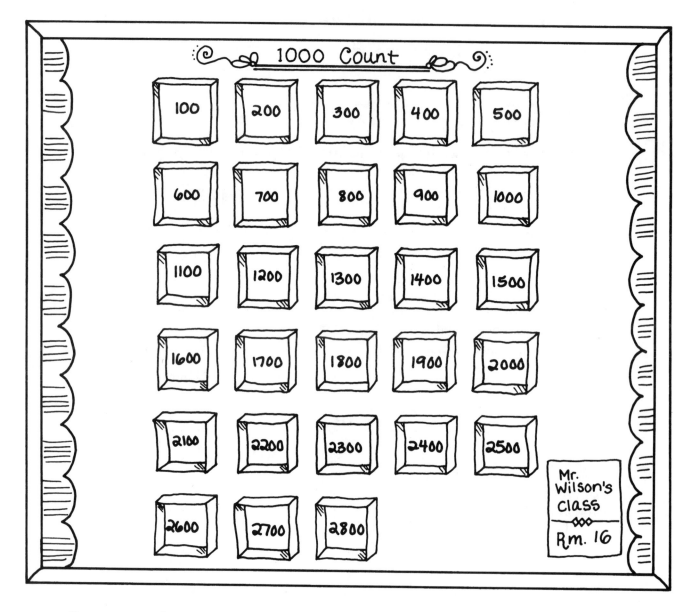

Suggestions

For additional activity ideas, see *Hands On Base Ten Blocks*, Creative Publications, Catalog Number 30159.

1000 COUNT

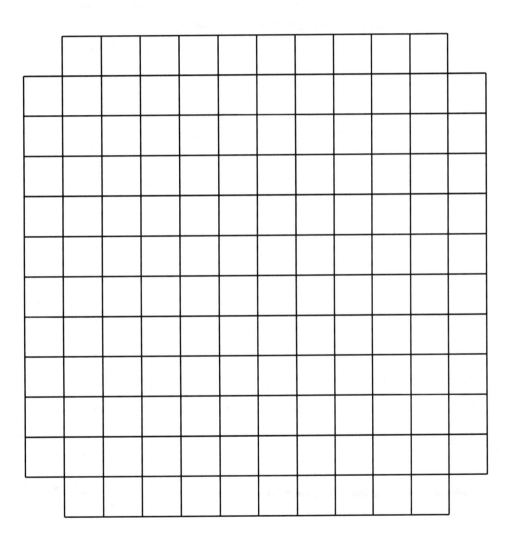

1000 Count Recording Sheet

Tangramarea

In this lesson, students create their own shapes, using some of the pieces from a set of tangrams. They find the areas of the shapes in terms of the small triangle and record by tracing around the pieces. Use to promote geometric thinking and to develop the concept of on-standard area

Classroom Organization

Eight groups of four sharing materials
Working independently

Materials

Each group of four students will need these materials:
4 sets of Tangrams • 8 copies of Tangramarea Recording Sheet, page 25

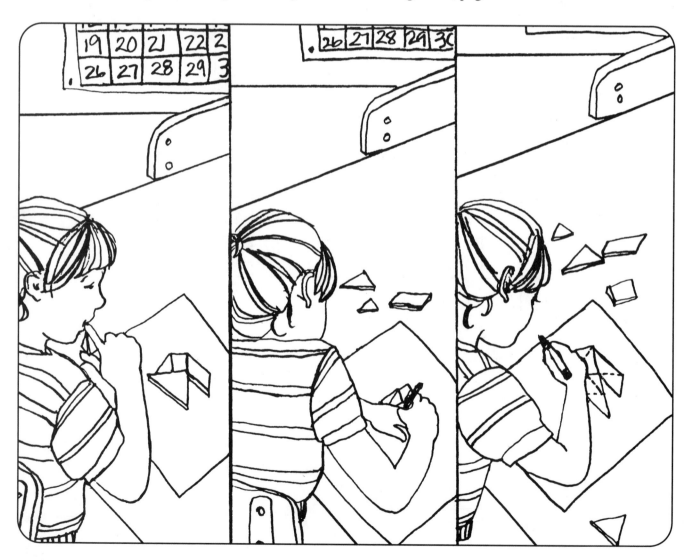

Introducing the Problem

Area is a measure of covering. Usually we find the area of a shape by finding out how many squares will cover it. Today we are going to find the area of shapes by covering them with triangles.

Do you think you can make shapes that have different areas?

Exploring with Tangrams

1. Tell the students to choose two pieces from their set of Tangrams and put them together to make a shape.

2. Tell the students to find out how many small triangles it takes to cover their shape. This number is the area of the shape in terms of small triangles. Have students tell about their shapes and areas.

Recording the Connection

1. Tell the students to make a different shape, using some of their Tangram pieces.

2. They should trace the shape onto their recording sheet.

3. Next, the students should find the area of their shape in terms of small triangles. They can use what they know about the area of different pieces to help them find this out.

4. They should trace in small triangle outlines on their shape to show the area.

5. Students should record the information about their shape and its area on the recording sheet.

Reporting and Displaying

When each student has had a chance to complete two recording sheets, collect them and display them where the students can see them. Tell the students that you want to organize the shapes into groups that are alike in some way. Ask the students for suggestions. Talk about the different ways you could organize the shapes, and choose one way.

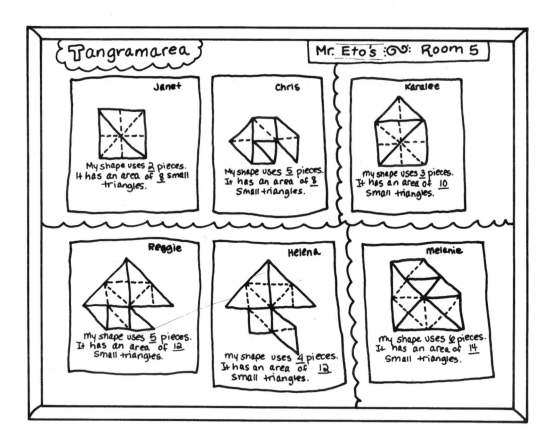

Solutions and Suggestions

There are many different shapes that students can make, using pieces from a Tangram set. The least area possible is one (the shape made with one small triangle), the greatest area possible is 16 (any shape made with all seven Tangram pieces). Students may suggest grouping shapes together that have the same area, or that have the same number of pieces, or that have the same number of pieces and the same area.

The classification aspect of this activity is as important as the completion of the recording sheets! Be sure to take advantage of it. One way to do this is to give all of the recording sheets to a small group of students and ask them to organize them and display them to show something they find interesting. When they have finished, ask them to write about what they did and then display this information with the recording sheets.

Tangramarea

Name _____

My shape uses _____ pieces.

It has an area of _____ small triangles.

Tangramarea Recording Sheet

Pentomino Challenge

In this lesson, students use Pattern Blocks squares to find the 12 pentomino shapes. They cut the shapes from the grid paper and sort them into two groups: those that will fold into topless boxes and those that will not. Use this lesson to develop geometric thinking.

Classroom Organization

Eight groups of four sharing materials
Working together

Materials

Each group of four students will need these materials:
• 5 orange Pattern Block squares • 4 copies of Pentomino Challenge Recording Sheet, page 29 • 1 large sheet of construction paper • Scissors and tape

Introducing the Problem

A pentomino is a shape made from five squares. The shapes are flat and whole sides of squares must touch.

These are O.K.

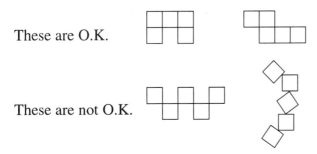

These are not O.K.

How long do you think it will take you to find all 12 pentomino shapes?

Exploring with Pattern Blocks

1. Students should arrange the squares and shade grid paper, tacking turns, until the group finds all 12 pentomino shapes.

2. Tell the students to cut out the shapes they discover. They should check the shapes carefully to make sure they are all different. If a shape can be flipped or turned to make another shape, it is not different.

3. Next, tell the students to predict which shapes they think will fold up to make topless boxes. Have them put the shapes into two groups: those they do not think will make boxes and those that they think will.

4. Have students fold their shapes to test their predictions.

Recording the Connection

1. Each group of students should work together to make a display of their work on the piece of construction paper.

2. They should write a description of what they did and what they found out from making pentominoes.

Reporting and Displaying

Post the different displays and discuss the interesting things they found out.

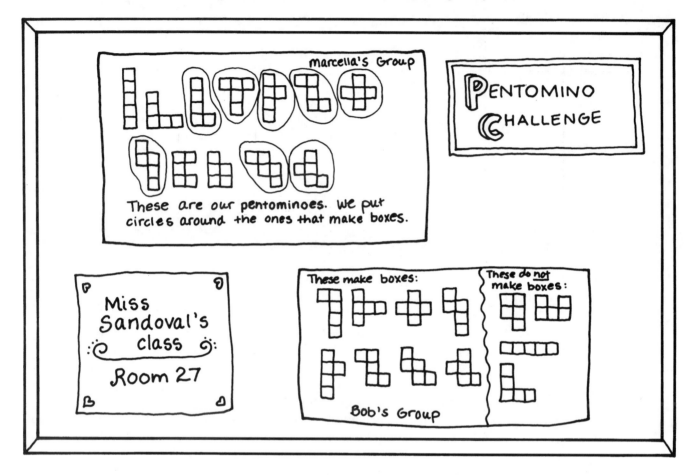

Solutions and Suggestions

These are 12 pentomino shapes. The circled shapes are the pentominoes that fold into boxes.

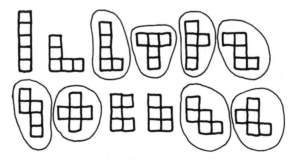

For more activity ideas, see *Pentomino Activities, Puzzles, and Lessons*, Creative Publications, Catalog Number 34482.

Pentomino Challenge

Permission is granted to reproduce this page.
Pentomino Challenge Recording Sheet

Pentomino Challenge 29

The Magic Decimal Point

In this lesson, students explore the relationships between the Base Ten Blocks, imagining what the next blocks in the sequence would be, both larger and smaller. They investigate how a number changes when different blocks are designated as one. Use to introduce the concept of decimals.

Classroom Organization

Eight groups of four sharing materials
Working together

Materials

Each group of four students will need these materials:
• Base Ten Blocks: 1 thousands-block, 1 hundreds-block, 9 tens-blocks, 9 ones-blocks, 4 copies of The Magic Decimal Point Recording Sheet, page 33 • 4 copies of Three-dimensional Base Ten Blocks, page 34 • 4 large sheets of construction paper • Paste

Introducing the Problem

You've been working with Base Ten Blocks and you know the values we have been using for each block.

Today we are going to work a magic trick and see how the blocks can change their values.

Exploring with Base Ten Blocks

1. Write the number and tell the students to show it with their blocks. Say, **We use the blocks to show this number and we agree that the value of this block** (the smallest cube) **is *one*. We know that we can keep building bigger blocks to show larger and larger numbers**.

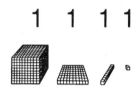

2. Ask, **What if we wanted to model a number smaller than one? What would the next smallest block look like?** Discuss the shape relationship of the blocks. Starting with the thousands-block, the shapes are cube, flat, stick, cube,...Ask, **What would the next smallest block look like?** (A little flat.) **What would its value be?** (One Tenth.) **What about the next smallest? The next?**

3. Say, **Now let's try the magic trick. What if we say the value off this block** (the stick) **is one. What is the name for each block now? If the stick is *one*, what is the value of this block** (point to the flat)? (Ten.) **What is the value of this block** (point to the large cube)? (One-hundred.) **And what is the value of this block** (point to the small cube)? (One-tenth.)

4. Continue to explore how the value of the blocks can change. Try calling the flat *one*. Then try calling the big cube *one*. Notice that the relationship between the blocks remains the same. Discuss that we write numbers that include numbers smaller than one, we write a decimal point to show which place in the number is the one's place.

5. Start with a different number (1137, for example) and repeat the above exploration. Now discuss what the value of each group is when different blocks are called *one*. For example, when the stick is called *one*, the group of small cubes is seven-tenths.

Recording the Connection

1. Students should represent a number with their blocks. They should paste three-dimensional blocks onto a piece of construction paper to match the blocks.

2. They should decide which block to call *one* and paste the magic decimal point (from the recording sheet) in the correct place.

3. They should complete the other three arrows, telling the value of each group of blocks.

4. Repeat for different numbers.

Reporting and Displaying

This lesson asks students to examine and consider the relationships inherent in the base-10 number system. Encourage each group to complete several of these pictures, then display them for the class to discuss. Take lots of time to talk about the students' thinking and the things that they found out. It will take time for the students to grasp some of the concepts in this lesson, but the time spent will be well worth the fundamental understandings that will be developed.

The Magic Decimal Point

Name _____

_____

Permission is granted to reproduce this page.
The Magical Decimal Point Recording Sheet

The Magic Decimal Point 33

Three Dimensional Base Ten Blocks

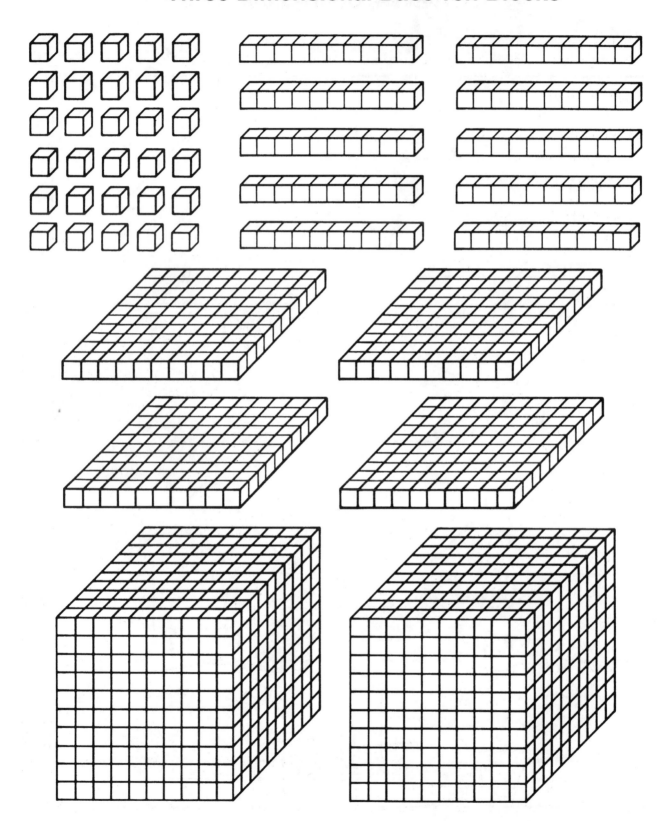

Rare Rectangles

In this lesson, students search for 16 different rectangles that can be made on a
5 × 5 geoboard. They record on dot paper, then think of ways to organize the many
solutions that the class has found. Use to promote visual thinking, problem solving,
and classification skills.

Classroom Organization

Eight groups of four sharing materials
Working in pairs

Materials

Each pair of students will need these materials:
• One 5 x 5 geoboard • 1 rubber band • 3 copies of Rare Rectangles Recording Sheet,
page 38 • Scissors

Introducing the Problem

You know that rectangles come in many different sizes and shapes. There are 16 different rectangles that can be made on a 5 × 5 geoboard.

How many do you think you can find?

Exploring with Geoboards

1. Tell the students to make a rectangle like the one shown on geoboards. Ask, **How many pegs does the rectangle touch?** (6) **How many pegs are inside?** (0)

2. Tell the students that they are going to find the 16 different rectangles that can be made on their geoboard. (Remember: Squares are rectangles.) Tell them that a rectangle is turned a different way or in a different place does not count as different.

Recording the Connection

1. Have students record the rectangles by drawing on dot paper on their recording sheets.

2. They should also record the number of pegs touched and the number of pegs inside each rectangle.

Reporting and Displaying

When each pair has finished searching for different rectangles, have them cut the squares apart to make separate recording sheets for each rectangle. Discuss some things the students found out about the rare rectangles. Ask the students to suggest ways to display the recording sheets. Choose one of the ways students suggest.

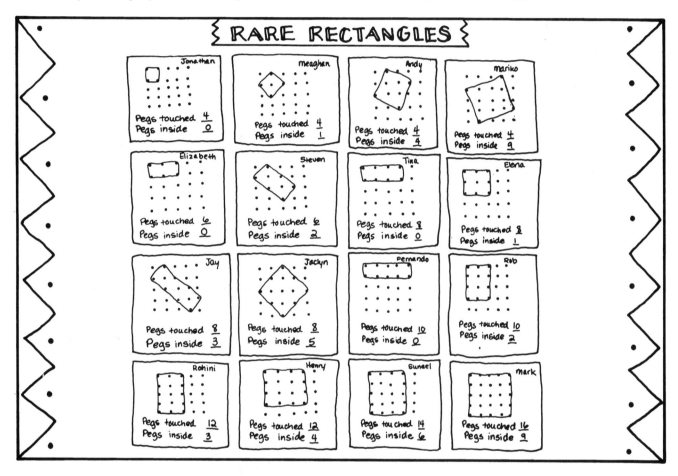

Solutions and Suggestions

There are many different ways to organize the rectangles found. Someone may suggest putting them in order from least to greatest number of pegs touched, or putting together all those with the same number inside.

They may want to put all the rectangles that are alike on top of each other for the display so only the 16 different ways are visible. Or, they may wish to arrange them to show the different positions (found by class) for the same rectangle on the geoboard.

For additional activity ideas, see *Moving On With Geoboards*, Creative Publications, Catalog Number 30492, and *Intermediate Jobcards™: Puzzles With Geoboards*, Catalog Number 34092.

Rare Rectangles

Names ________________

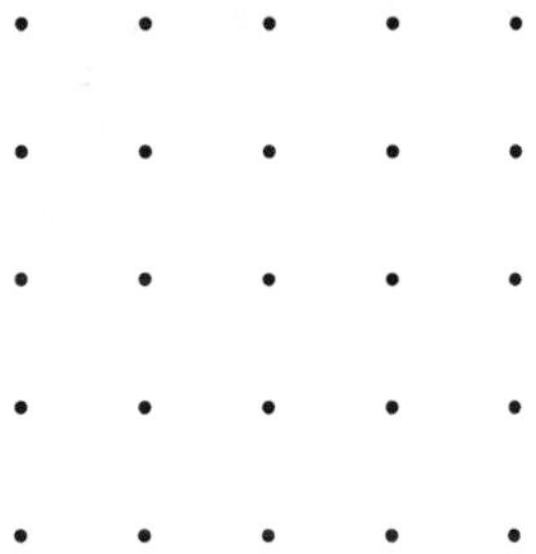

Pegs touched ________
Pegs inside ________

Names ________________

Pegs touched ________
Pegs inside ________

Names ________________

Pegs touched ________
Pegs inside ________

Names ________________

Pegs touched ________
Pegs inside ________

Names ________________

Pegs touched ________
Pegs inside ________

Names ________________

Pegs touched ________
Pegs inside ________

Rare Rectangles Recording Sheet

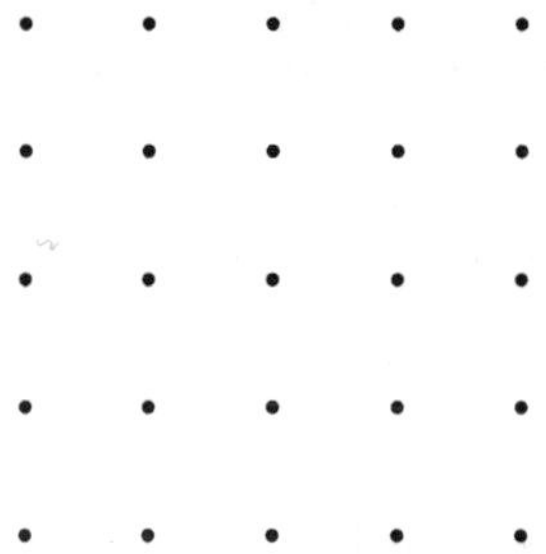

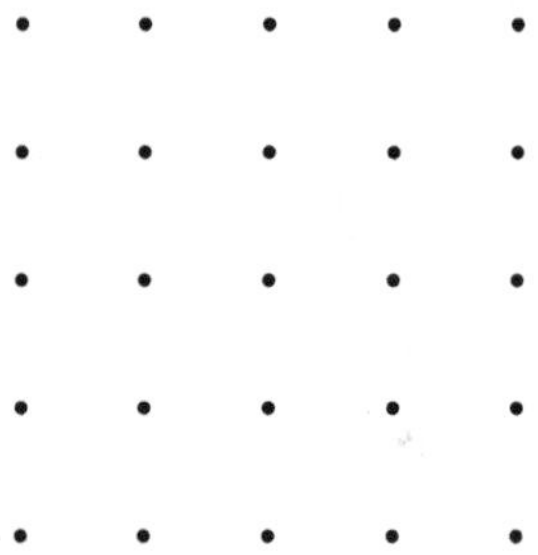

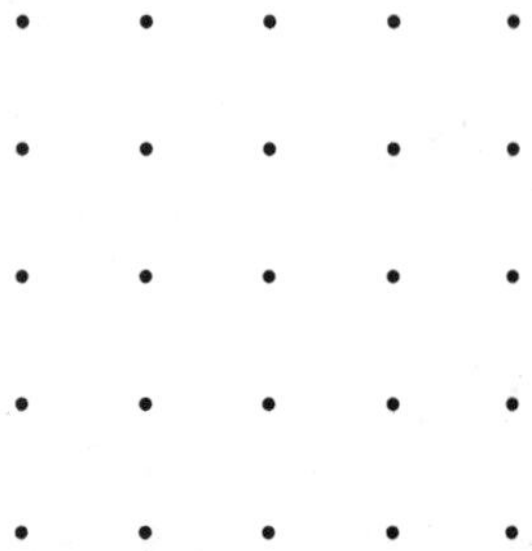

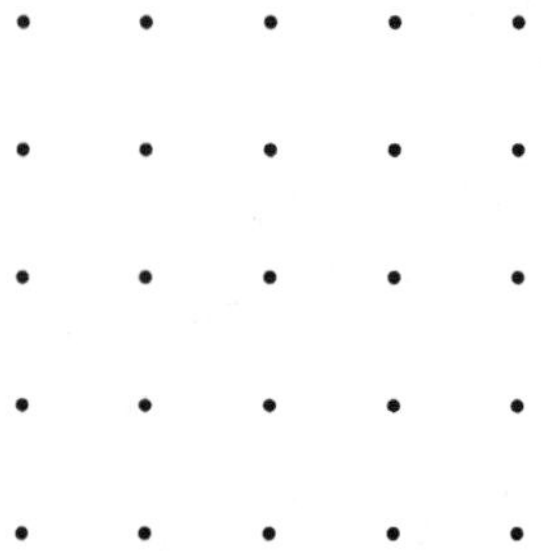

Rainbow Squares and Cubes

In this lesson, students use Rainbow Cubes to build all the square and cube numbers between 1 and 100. Each group organizes their own work and writes a description of what they did. Building squares and cubes this way allows students to construct a powerful mental image of square and cube numbers.

Classroom Organization

Eight groups of four sharing materials
Working together

Materials

Each group of four students will need these materials :
• 100 Cubes: If you have the Connections Kit, use 75 Rainbow Cubes™ and 25 Base Ten ones-blocks • 1 copy of Rainbow Squares and Cubes Recording Sheet, page 42 • 6 copies of Centimeter Grid Paper, Page 43 • Scissors, crayons, and tape

Introducing the Problem

When we multiply a number by itself, we call the product the square of the number. When we multiply a number by itself and then by itself again, we call the product the cube of the number.

How can you tell if the number is a square or a cube?

Exploring with Rainbow Cubes

1. Have students look at the recording sheet and the numbers 1-100. Say, **Look at the number 9. If you can make a square using nine blocks, then the number nine is a square number.** Have students take nine blocks and try to make the square.

2. Say, **What multiplication equation tells about this square?** (3×3)

3. Next, work with the number 8. Say, **Can you make a square with eight cubes?** (No) **Can you make a cube?** (Yes.) **Eight is a cube number. Ask, What multiplication equation tells about this cube?** ($2 \times 2 \times 2$)

4. Tell the groups that their job is to find all the square and cube numbers between 1 and 100 and write the multiplication equation that describes them.

Recording the Connection

1. As the groups begin to investigate the numbers on the hundreds chart, tell them that they must make a drawing or model of each square and cube they find. They may use the hundreds chart, the centimeter grid paper, and the scissors, tape, and crayons to help them record their work.

2. When they have recorded all the squares and cubes, they should write a summary of what they did so they can tell the rest of the class what they found out.

Reporting And Displaying

Have the different groups report to the class what they found out in their investigation. You may want to display the different group reports on a bulletin board.

Rainbow Squares and Cubes

Carrie's Group

These are the square numbers we found.

These are the cube numbers we found.

Solutions

Square Numbers Between 1 and 100

$1 \times 1 = 1$	$4 \times 4 = 16$	$7 \times 7 = 49$
$2 \times 2 = 4$	$5 \times 5 = 25$	$8 \times 8 = 64$
$3 \times 3 = 9$	$6 \times 6 = 36$	$9 \times 9 = 81$

Cube Numbers Between 1 and 100

$1 \times 1 \times 1 = 1$	$3 \times 3 \times 3 = 27$
$2 \times 2 \times 2 = 8$	$4 \times 4 \times 4 = 64$

Rainbow Squares and Cubes

Name _____

1	2	3	4	5	6	7	8	9	10
11	12	13	14	15	16	17	18	19	20
21	22	23	24	25	26	27	28	29	30
31	32	33	34	35	36	37	38	39	40
41	42	43	44	45	46	47	48	49	50
51	52	53	54	55	56	57	58	59	60
61	62	63	64	65	66	67	68	69	70
71	72	73	74	75	76	77	78	79	80
81	82	83	84	85	86	87	88	89	90
91	92	93	94	95	96	97	98	99	100

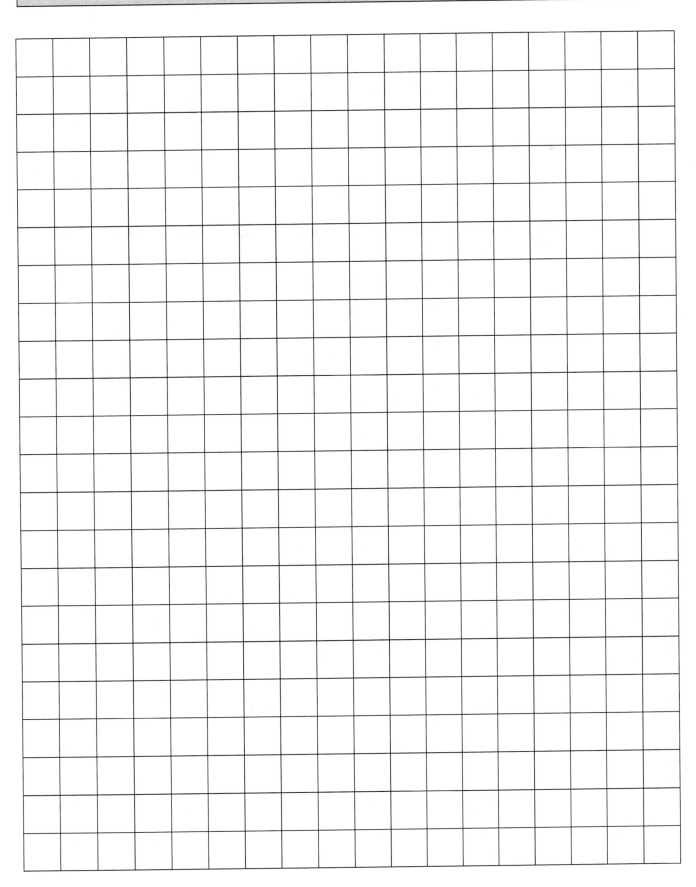

1-Centimeter Grid

Rainbow Factors

In this lesson, students use Rainbow Cubes to explore the concept of greatest common factor. They construct rectangles to show factors of two different numbers and then compare the factor lists to determine the greatest common factor. Use during a fraction chapter to introduce the concept of greatest common factor.

Classroom Organization

Eight groups of four sharing materials
Working in pairs

Materials

Each group of four students will need these materials:
•112 centimeter cubes (75 Rainbow Cubes™ and 37 Base Ten ones-blocks, if you are using the Connections Kit) • 6 copies of Rainbow Factors Recording Sheet, page 47

Introducing the Problem

Sometimes you need to know the greatest common factor that two numbers have in common. This is especially important when you are trying to reduce a fraction to its lowest terms. Today we are going to explore a way for determining the greatest common factor of two numbers.

What number do you think is the greatest common factor for 6 and 9?

Exploring with Rainbow Cubes™

1. Have students work with a partner. Tell them to place one recording sheet between them.

2. One student should make all the possible rectangles for the number 6 (1 x 6, 2 x 3) and the other student should make all the rectangles for 9 (1 x 9, 3 x 3).

3. Display the rectangles the students made and write the multiplication equations.

$$1 \times 6 \qquad 2 \times 3 \qquad\qquad 1 \times 9 \qquad 3 \times 3$$

4. Ask students to tell you the factors of 6 and 9 as you write them on the chalkboard

   Factors of 6: 1, 2, 3, 6   Factors of 9: 1, 3, 9

5. Have the class examine the list and determine the common factors. (1, 3) Then ask which of these common factors is the greatest. (3)

Recording the Connection

1. Show the students how to record by drawing pictures of rectangles they made with their cubes and writing the multiplication equation for each rectangle. They should list the factors of each number, the common factors and the greatest common factor.

2. Challenge the partners to choose other pairs of numbers and find their greatest common factors using their Rainbow Cubes.

3. Each pair of students should try to complete six pairs of numbers.

Reporting And Displaying

Have students display their work on a bulletin board and share with the rest of the class what they found out about greatest common factors. Talk about some interesting ways to organize the information they have collected. Which pair of these numbers have the most common factors? Which had the least? Put together all the number pairs with the same number as greatest common factor. Which number was found most frequently as GCF? Which was found least frequently?

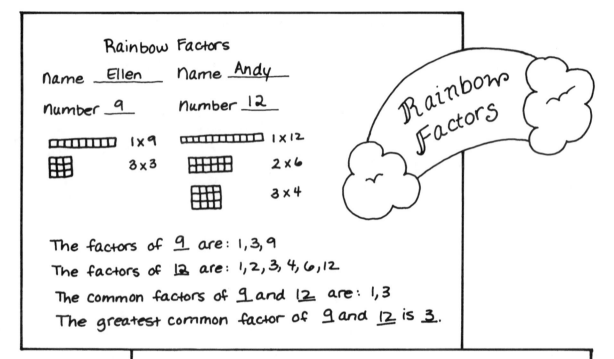

Rainbow Factors

Name __Ellen__   Name __Andy__

number __9__   number __12__

⬚⬚⬚⬚⬚ 1 x 9   ⬚⬚⬚⬚⬚⬚ 1 x 12
▦ 3 x 3   ▦ 2 x 6
                 ▦ 3 x 4

The factors of __9__ are: 1, 3, 9
The factors of __12__ are: 1, 2, 3, 4, 6, 12
The common factors of __9__ and __12__ are: 1, 3
The greatest common factor of __9__ and __12__ is __3__.

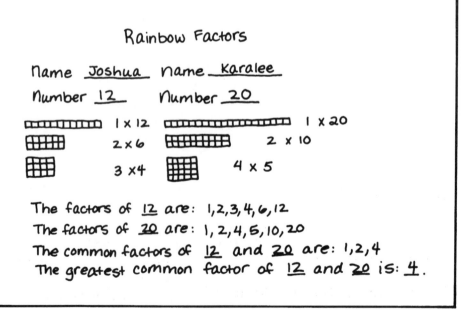

Rainbow Factors

Name __Joshua__   Name __Karalee__

Number __12__   Number __20__

⬚⬚⬚⬚⬚ 1 x 12   ⬚⬚⬚⬚⬚⬚ 1 x 20
▦ 2 x 6   ▦ 2 x 10
▦ 3 x 4   ▦ 4 x 5

The factors of __12__ are: 1, 2, 3, 4, 6, 12
The factors of __20__ are: 1, 2, 4, 5, 10, 20
The common factors of __12__ and __20__ are: 1, 2, 4
The greatest common factor of __12__ and __20__ is: __4__.

Rainbow Factors

Name ______________________ Name ____________________

Number ____________________ Number __________________

The factors of _________ are:

The factors of _________ are:

The common factors of _________ and _________ are:

The greatest common factor of _________ and _________ is:

Rainbow Factors Recording Sheet

Make A Million

In this lesson, use Base Ten Blocks and their understanding of place value concepts to describe what it would take to make a model of a million. They clarify their thinking by putting their plan in writing. Use this lesson to enrich place value understandings and to help students construct their own personal image of what a million means.

Classroom Organization

Eight groups of four sharing materials
Working together

Materials

Each group of four students will need these materials:
• Base Ten Blocks: 1 thousands-block, 1 hundreds-block, 18 tens-blocks, 37 ones-blocks • 1 copy of Make A Million Recording Sheet, page 51 • Blank paper

Introducing the Problem

You know you don't have a million blocks in your set, but what if you wanted to show a model of a million?

What would you need in order to show that?

Exploring with Base Ten Blocks

1. Have students work together to sort out their Base Ten Blocks into like groups: ones, tens, hundreds, thousands. Have them put the blocks in order.

2. Review the names of the different types of blocks: ones, tens, hundreds, thousands. Discuss with them the relationship between the blocks. Students should notice that each block is ten times greater than the next smallest block.

3. Challenge the groups to use what they know about the blocks to figure out what a million-block would look like. What shape would it be? What would its dimensions be? How do they know?

Recording the Connection

1. Have each group write about how they figured out the problem, including a sketch of their millions-block.

2. Insist that students prove their solution is correct in their written report. A sketch alone is good but it is not sufficient.

Reporting and Displaying

Allow the different groups to report to the class what their solution to the problem was and how they reached the conclusions they did. Display the different reports on a special *Make A Million* bulletin board.

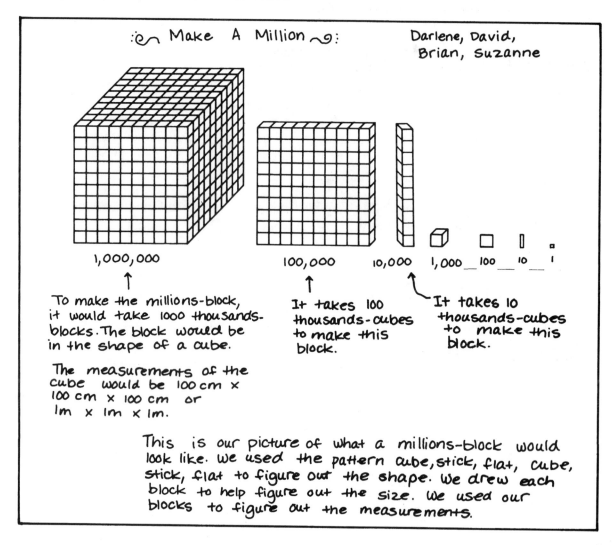

Solutions and Suggestions

If there were a millions-block in the Base Ten Blocks set, it would be in the shape of a cube and would take up one cubic meter of space. Another way to think of it would be 1000 thousands-cubes. As a class, you may want to build a model off this cube. Use six large sheets of paper 1 meter × 1 meter. Tape the paper together to make a cube.

What about a billions-block? It's a cube made of 1000 millions-cubes. Its dimensions are : 10 meters × 10 meters × 10 meters (approximately 30 feet × 30 feet × 30 feet). It would not fit in your classroom.

Make A Million

Names_____

_____

We think the millions-block will look like this:

This is the way we figured it out:

20 Thinking Questions

How can you sort your Treasures?

Take out your Treasures. How can you sort them into piles of Treasures that are alike? Tell how you sorted them. Use pictures, words, and numbers to make a report. Show how many Treasures are in each group.

MATERIALS

For each pair of students

- Sorting Treasures (approximately 50 of one kind)
- paper, pencils, and crayons for recording

INTRODUCING THE QUESTION

1 Tell students they will be sorting their Treasures into groups of Treasures that are alike. **Take out your Treasures. Decide with your partner on a way to sort them. How can you sort your Treasures into piles or groups of Treasures that are alike?**

2 When partners finish sorting, they should count the number of Treasures in each group and make a report. **Tell how you sorted your Treasures. Use pictures, words, and numbers to make a report. Show how many Treasures are in each group.**

WHAT SHOULD YOU DO IF . . .

▶ Some students pick a sorting method that creates many piles or a method that creates only two piles?

This is okay. Be sure students can explain clearly what their sorting method is. It will be beneficial later during the class discussion to talk about why some sorting methods create many piles and other methods create only two piles.

▶ Some students start dividing Treasures into piles without using a sorting strategy?

Ask students to explain what sorting method they are using. They may have a method that is not obvious to you. Also, some students may sort using more than one attribute—for example, a pile of yellow creepy crawlers, a pile of 4-legged creepy crawlers, and a pile of short creepy crawlers. Accept any method as long as students can explain clearly how they are sorting.

▶ Some students don't like their Treasures and want to sort another pair's Treasures?

This is natural. Some students will prefer sorting creepy crawlers instead of tiles, for example. Plan on doing this activity with your students more than once, and tell students that they will have a chance to sort a different Treasure next time.

WHAT YOU MIGHT SEE

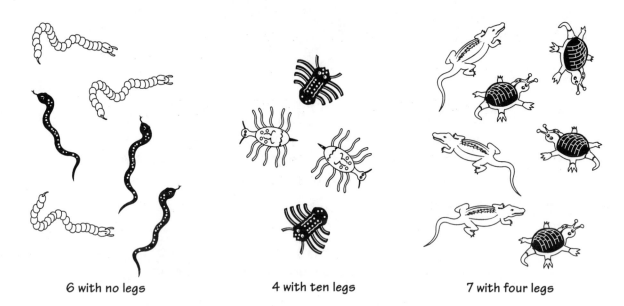

6 with no legs   4 with ten legs   7 with four legs

Some students may sort their creepy crawlers by the number of legs.

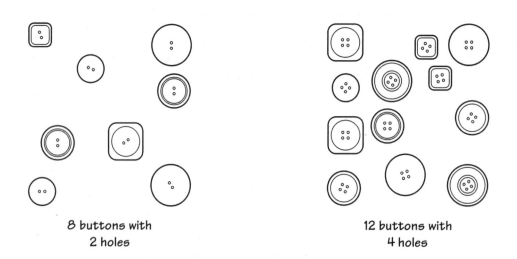

8 buttons with
2 holes

12 buttons with
4 holes

Some students may sort their buttons by the number of holes.

WHAT TO LOOK FOR IN STUDENT'S WORK

Was the student able to sort the Treasures into groups?

Was the student able to count how many Treasures were in each group?

Did the student record how she sorted the Treasures?

QUESTIONS FOR DISCUSSION

- How did you sort your Treasures? How many Treasures were in each group?

- Did anyone sort the Treasures in a different way? Tell what you did.

- Do you think there are more or fewer ways to sort the tiles than there are to sort the creepy crawlers?

- Do you think it is easier to sort the shells or the buttons by color? Tell us why.

- Do you think there are many different ways to sort the Treasures? What makes you think so?

- Of all the ways you found to sort your Treasures, which ways wouldn't work if you couldn't see them?

JOURNAL REFLECTION

Write how you sorted your Treasures.

Suppose you were going to sort your Treasures in another way. How would you do it?

How are the two buttons alike and different?

Pick any two buttons. Can you describe how the buttons are alike and how they are different? Make a drawing of your buttons. Write about how they are alike and how they are different.

MATERIALS

For each pair of students

- Sorting Treasures (buttons)
- paper, pencils, and crayons for recording

INTRODUCING THE QUESTION

1 Hold up two different books in front of the class. **How are these objects alike? How are they different?** On the chalkboard or overhead projector, make lists of the words the students use to describe the similarities and the differences. Leave the lists up during the activity.

2 Introduce the question. **Work with your partner. Choose any two buttons from your pile. Can you describe how your buttons are alike and how they are different? Make a drawing of your buttons. Write about how they are alike and how they are different.**

WHAT SHOULD YOU DO IF . . .

▶ Some students list only one difference and one similarity for their two buttons?

These students may think that there aren't very many differences or similarities to be found with only two objects. Encourage these students to stretch their thinking. Help students focus on the different attributes. **Describe this button to me. Can you describe this button in the same way? Explain.**

▶ Some students find only differences between the buttons?

These students may be so focused on listing all the differences, they forget to look for similarities. Remind them that they must also describe how the two buttons are alike.

▶ Some students have difficulty describing how their buttons are alike and different?

These students may not yet have the language skills needed to write how the buttons are alike and different. Encourage these students to draw pictures to show the buttons' similarities and differences.

WHAT YOU MIGHT SEE

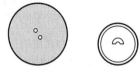

They are both round. The orange button is bigger.

Some students may find only one similarity and one difference.

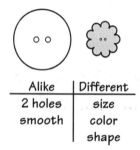

Alike	Different
2 holes	size
smooth	color
	shape

Some students may use a table to organize the similarities and differences.

WHAT TO LOOK FOR IN STUDENT'S WORK

Was the student able to find more than one similarity and one difference?

Does the student's recording show clearly the similarities and differences?

QUESTIONS FOR DISCUSSION

- In how many ways are your two buttons alike? What are the ways?

- In how many ways are your buttons different? What are the ways?

- Did anyone come up with another way to compare their two buttons? Explain the differences and similarities you found.

- Now that you have heard how others compared their buttons, could you come up with more similarities and differences between your two buttons? What are they?

JOURNAL REFLECTION

Would it be easier or more difficult to compare three buttons? Why do you think so?

Explain how you would compare the two buttons if you could not see them.

How many Treasures do you have?

Organize your Treasures so that you can tell how many you have without counting by ones. How many Treasures do you have? Make a recording to explain how you organized your Treasures.

MATERIALS

For each pair of students

- Sorting Treasures (approximately 100)
- paper, pencils, and crayons for recording

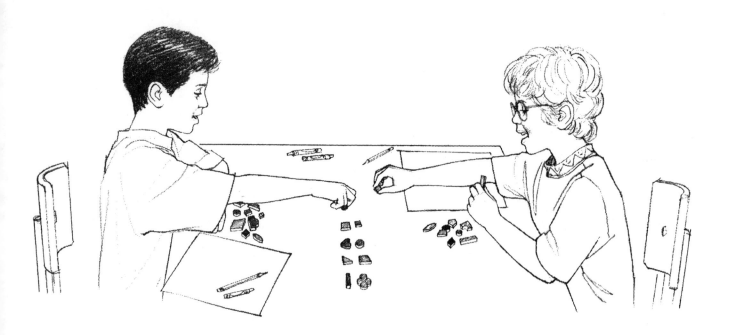

INTRODUCING THE QUESTION

1 Engage the class in a discussion about the different ways to count objects. **How might you count the number of shoes in the room without counting them one at a time? What are some other ways you could count objects without counting by ones? How did you figure that out?** Give students plenty of time to talk about different counting methods.

2 Introduce the question to the class. **Work with your partner. Organize your Treasures so you don't have to count them by ones. How many Treasures do you have? Make a recording. Explain how you organized your Treasures.**

WHAT SHOULD YOU DO IF . . .

▶ Some students organize their Treasures but still count them by ones?

Some students may not be confident with their total unless they count the Treasures by ones. Accept this method. These students may simply need more experience counting groups of objects.

▶ Some students focus on organizing the Treasures but miscalculate the number they have?

These students may organize the Treasures into groups that are not easy for them to count. For example, they may organize the objects in groups of 7 and have difficulty counting by sevens. This will be valuable information for the class discussion, when students talk about which numbers are easier to count by.

▶ Some students are uncertain about how to organize their Treasures and look to see how other groups are organizing their objects?

Some students may need reassurance on how to organize the Treasures. Encourage the students to discuss with each other how they might group the Treasures.

WHAT YOU MIGHT SEE

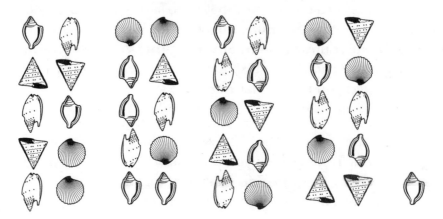

41 shells in all

Some students may quickly organize their Treasures into groups of 10.

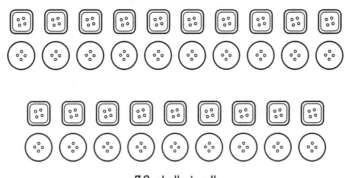

38 shells in all

Some students may organize their Treasures into groups of 2.

WHAT TO LOOK FOR IN STUDENT'S WORK

Was the student able to find the total number of Treasures?

Was the student able to organize her Treasures in order to tell how many she had without counting by ones?

Was the student able to explain clearly how he organized his Treasures?

QUESTIONS FOR DISCUSSION

- How many Treasures did you have in all?

- How did you organize your Treasures so you could tell how many you had without counting them by ones?

- Did anyone organize their Treasures in a different way? How?

- Was it easy or difficult to find the total using your way? Explain.

- Which way do you think would be easiest to find the total?

- How many ways can you organize your Treasures so you can tell how many you have without counting them by ones? What makes you think so?

JOURNAL REFLECTION

Why might it be helpful sometimes to figure out how many objects you have without counting them by ones?

How could you figure out the number of students in your class without counting them by ones?

What does a design worth 20 look like?

Use your Pattern Blocks. Suppose a green triangle equals 1, a blue rhombus equals 2, a red trapezoid equals 3, and a yellow hexagon equals 6. What does a design worth 20 look like? Make a design. Record your design. Write how you know it is worth 20.

MATERIALS

For each pair of students

- Pattern Blocks
- paper, pencils, and crayons for recording

For the overhead projector

- Pattern Blocks

INTRODUCING THE QUESTION

1   Write on the chalkboard: green = 1, blue = 2, red = 3, and yellow = 6. **Suppose the blocks have these values. Can you make a design worth 5?** Give students time to work.

2   Let volunteers show their designs on the overhead. **Tell us about your design. How do you know your design is worth 5?** Let students explain how they arrived at their answers.

3   Introduce the question to the class. **Can you and your partner make a design worth 20? What would it look like? Make a recording of your design. Write how you know it is worth 20.**

4   When students are finished, have them walk around the class and look at other students' designs.

WHAT SHOULD YOU DO IF . . .

▶ Some students make a design that isn't worth 20?

These students may be more concerned with making an interesting design. Let students explore different designs for a while, then focus their attention on the question. **What is the value of your design? How can you find out?**

▶ Students don't have enough blocks to use all of one type?

Students won't have enough blocks to make designs using only one type of block. Encourage students to use other types of blocks as well. **Can you make a design using more than one type of block?**

▶ Some students make designs that are not "flat"?

Students may make designs where blocks are stacked or standing up versus lying down. Encourage this creative thinking. Students may, however, have difficulty recording these designs on paper. Let them make an attempt at representing their work. The thinking process involved is more important than the final product.

WHAT YOU MIGHT SEE

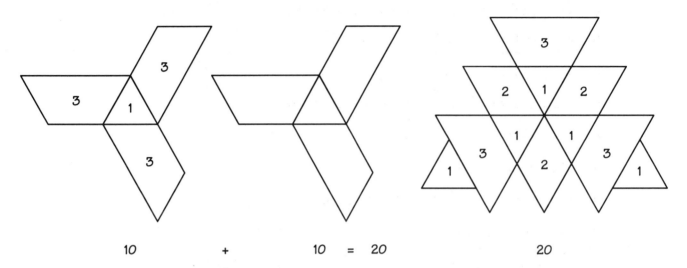

10   +   10   =   20   20

Some students may make a shape worth 10 and repeat the shape to make a design worth 20.

Some students may make a more elaborate design in which they need to add the value of each individual block to find the total value of the design.

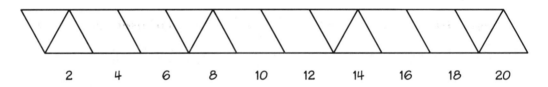

2   4   6   8   10   12   14   16   18   20

Some students may make a pattern in which they can easily count by twos to 20.

WHAT TO LOOK FOR IN STUDENT'S WORK

Was the student able to make a design worth 20?

Was the student able to explain clearly how she figured the value of her design?

Was the student able to make a recording of his design?

QUESTIONS FOR DISCUSSION

- What does your design worth 20 look like?

- How did you figure the value of your design?

- Who made a different design worth 20? What does it look like?

- How did you figure the value of your design?

- How did you begin this problem?

- Did someone start a different way?

- How many blocks did you use to create your design?

- Did anyone create a design using more/fewer blocks?

- Who made a design with the fewest blocks? Which blocks did you use?

- Who made a design with the most blocks? Which blocks did you use?

JOURNAL REFLECTION

Would you need more blue blocks or yellow blocks to make a design worth 20? Explain your answer.

_____ green blocks = 3 red blocks. Draw a picture to show your answer.

Suppose a friend wanted to trade you 3 blue blocks for 1 yellow block. Is the trade fair? Explain why or why not.

How many tables would we need?

Use your Pattern Blocks. Suppose an orange square stands for a table that seats 4 students. How many tables would we need for the class? Record your work. Explain how you know how many tables we would need.

MATERIALS

For each pair of students

- Pattern Blocks (orange and green)
- paper, pencils, and crayons for recording

For the overhead projector

- Pattern Blocks (orange and green)

INTRODUCING THE QUESTION

1   Show an orange block with 4 green triangles on the overhead projector. The orange block will represent a table and the green blocks will represent chairs.

Suppose this orange block stands for a table that can seat 4 people. How many tables would we need for 8 people? (2) **How do you know?** Give students time to share their explanations.

2   Leave the Pattern Blocks on the overhead with the light on so that students can refer to it while they work. Introduce the question to the class. **Work with your partner. Use your Pattern Blocks to help. How many tables would we need for the class if every table seats 4 students? Record your work. Write how you know how many tables we would need.**

WHAT SHOULD YOU DO IF . . .

▶ Some students have difficulty determining how many students are in the class?

You may wish to tell everyone how many students there are in the class when introducing the problem, and then tell the class how many students are absent. The emphasis here is not on being able to count how many students are in the class but on figuring out how many tables are needed.

▶ Some students don't count the last table that may have 3 or fewer students?

If the number of students in the class is not divisible by 4, there will be one table that seats 3 or fewer students. Some students may not consider this a "complete" table and may not count it. Use this information to prompt a discussion. **How many tables did you come up with? How many students in all can sit at the tables? How many students are there in our class? Where do the "extra" students sit?**

WHAT YOU MIGHT SEE

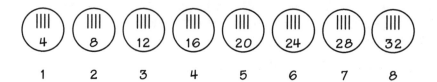

Some students may skip count by fours until they reach the number of students in the class, then count the number of groups of 4.

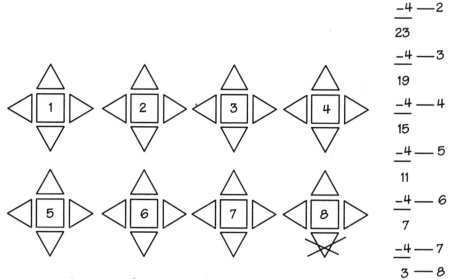

```
31
-4 —1
27
-4 —2
23
-4 —3
19
-4 —4
15
-4 —5
11
-4 —6
7
-4 —7
3 —8
```

Some students may draw pictures of tables and chairs until there are enough for the class.

Some students may use repeated subraction to find the number of groups of 4.

WHAT TO LOOK FOR IN STUDENT'S WORK

Was the student able to find how many tables the class would need?

Did the student explain clearly how she found how many tables the class would need?

Was the student able to make a recording of his work?

QUESTIONS FOR DISCUSSION

- How many tables would our class need? How do you know?

- Did anyone get a different number?

- How did you solve the problem?

- Did anyone use skip counting to help solve the problem? Tell how you used it.

- Were there 4 students sitting at each table?

- How would you change the way you solved the problem if our class had 100 students?

- How would you figure it out for tables that seat 3? How about 2?

- How many students would have to sit at each table if we had only 2 tables?

JOURNAL REFLECTION

Describe how you would solve this problem for tables that seated 8 students.

Suppose 6 new students joined our class. How many tables would we need now? Explain your answer.

How many tables for 2 would you need for your family? Draw a picture to explain your answer.

Is it true?

Use your Base Ten Blocks. Are these statements true? Record how you know if the statements are true or not.

even number + even number = even number
odd number + odd number = odd number
even number + odd number = even number

MATERIALS

For each pair of students

- Base Ten Blocks
- paper and pencils for recording

For the overhead projector

- Base Ten Blocks (15 ones)

INTRODUCING THE QUESTION

1 Show 14 ones blocks on the overhead projector. **Is the value of these blocks even or odd?** (even) **How do you know?** Now add 1 block to the 14. **Is the value of these blocks even or odd?** (odd) **How do you know?**

2 Tell the students that they will be working on combinations of even and odd numbers. **Use your Base Ten Blocks. Are these statements true? Record how you know if the statements are true or not.**

> **even number + even number = even number**
> **odd number + odd number = odd number**
> **even number + odd number = even number**

WHAT SHOULD YOU DO IF . . .

▶ Some students are having difficulty understanding how to start working on the problem?

These students may be unclear as to how the sentences can relate to numbers. **Name two even numbers. If you add those two numbers together, will you get an odd or an even number? How might you use this information to help you with these statements?**

▶ Some students use one example to prove or disprove each statement?

Although it is a hard concept to get across to students, one example is not enough to prove or disprove a statement. Two examples is minimal, and three or more examples is better. Challenge them to search further. **How confident are you that you've done enough work? Would another person be convinced by the data you've collected?**

▶ Some students complete the task with the blocks but are confused about how to record their findings?

If students use many examples, they may need help organizing the data. Have these students orally explain to each other what they have done with the blocks. **How can you organize your work to show what you've found?**

WHAT YOU MIGHT SEE

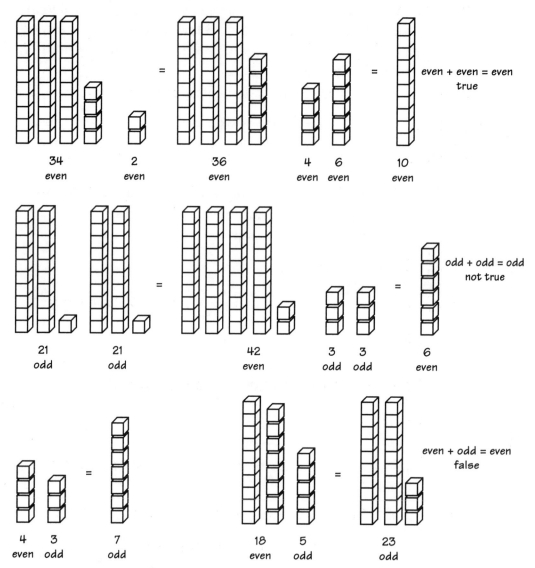

34   2   =   36   4   6   =   10   even + even = even
even   even   even   even   even   even   true

21   21   =   42   3   3   =   6   odd + odd = odd
odd   odd   even   odd   odd   even   not true

4   3   =   7   18   5   =   23   even + odd = even
even   odd   odd   even   odd   odd   false

Some students may find two or more examples to prove or disprove each statement.

WHAT TO LOOK FOR IN STUDENT'S WORK

Was the student able to find examples to prove or disprove each statement?

Did the student find "even number + even number = even number" to be true? Did the student find "odd number + odd number = odd number" and "even number + odd number = even number" to be false?

Was the student able to make a recording of his work?

Was the student's recording for this activity clear and descriptive?

QUESTIONS FOR DISCUSSION

- How did you begin to work on this problem? Do you think that was a good way to begin? Why?

- Which statements are true? Which statements are false?

- How did you prove which statements are true and which are false?

- How did you organize your work?

- Did anyone organize their work a different way? Tell us about it.

- If you were asked to do this activity again, would you do it the same way? If not, how would you do it differently?

JOURNAL REFLECTION

Is 13 + 11 an odd or an even answer? Tell how you know.

Is this statement true or false? Tell how you know.

odd number + even number = even number

Do you think these statements are true for all even and odd numbers? Explain.

How many should you get?

Suppose I have 53 stamps and you have 19 stamps.
How many stamps should I give you so we both have
the same number? Use your Base Ten Blocks to
prove your answer. Make a recording that explains
how you know how many stamps you need.

MATERIALS

For each pair of students

- Base Ten Blocks
- paper and pencils for recording

For the overhead projector

- Base Ten Blocks (10 ones)

INTRODUCING THE QUESTION

```
     □       □ □ □
  □ □       □ □ □ □
  3 ones       7 ones
```

1 Show a group of 3 ones blocks and a group of 7 ones blocks on the overhead projector. **How many blocks are in each group?** (3, 7) **Suppose you wanted both groups to have the same number of blocks. What would you do?** (Take 2 ones blocks from the group of 7 and give them to the group of 3 so that both groups have 5 blocks.) **How many blocks would there be in each group?** (5)

2 Introduce the question to the class. **Suppose I have 53 stamps and you have 19 stamps. How many stamps should I give you so we both have the same number? Use your Base Ten Blocks to prove your answer. Make a recording that explains how you know how many stamps you need.**

WHAT SHOULD YOU DO IF...

▶ Some students add 34 stamps to 19 so both have 53 stamps?

These students may have misunderstood the question. Ask them to explain the problem. **How many stamps do I have? How many stamps do you have? What does the problem ask? What did you do?**

▶ Some students find that both will have 36 stamps, but they don't explain how many stamps were exchanged?

These students have worked the problem but have not answered the specific question. **Look at the problem again. What does it ask? How can you answer it?**

▶ Some students find the answer without using their Base Ten Blocks?

Ask these students to prove their answer using Base Ten Blocks. **How can you use Base Ten Blocks to prove your answer?**

WHAT YOU MIGHT SEE

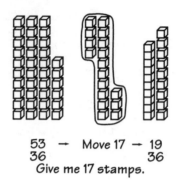

53 → Move 17 → 19
36   36
Give me 17 stamps.

Some students may move 1 block from the group of 53 to the group of 19 until each group has the same number of blocks. Then they may count to find that 17 blocks were exchanged.

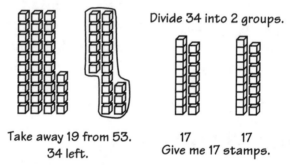

Divide 34 into 2 groups.

Take away 19 from 53.
34 left.

17   17
Give me 17 stamps.

Some students may take away 19 blocks from 53 blocks and divide the difference into 2 groups of 17 blocks.

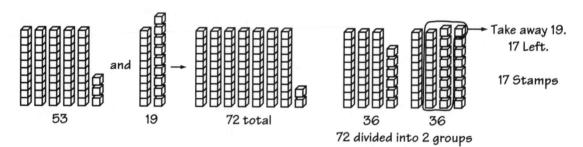

53   19   72 total   36   36

Take away 19.
17 Left.

17 Stamps

72 divided into 2 groups

Some students may find a total of 72 blocks, divide 72 into 2 equal groups of 36 blocks, and then may take away 19 blocks to find how many stamps were given.

WHAT TO LOOK FOR IN STUDENT'S WORK

Was the student able to find that 17 stamps need to be given so both would have the same number?

Was the student able to make a recording that explains how she solved the problem?

Did the student use Base Ten Blocks to prove his answer?

QUESTIONS FOR DISCUSSION

- How many stamps should I give you so we both have the same number?

- Did anyone get a different answer? What was your answer?

- How did you solve the problem?

- Did anyone solve the problem in a different way? How?

- How did you use your Base Ten Blocks to prove your answer?

- What would happen if I had 54 stamps and you had 19 stamps? How many stamps should I give you so we have the same number? Explain your answer.

JOURNAL REFLECTION

Suppose you have 13 stamps, a friend has 27 stamps, and another friend has 20 stamps. How many stamps would you need to give each other so everyone has the same number? Explain how you solved this problem.

Suppose, instead of having 53 stamps and 19 stamps, there were 63 stamps and 29 stamps. Would the answer change? Explain your thinking.

Did using Base Ten Blocks help you understand the problem better? Explain why or why not.

How many different shapes can you make?

How many different shapes can you make with four Rainbow Cubes? First make a prediction, then try to find as many different shapes as you can. Record each shape. Write about your prediction, and explain how you know you found all the possible shapes.

MATERIALS

For each pair of students

- Rainbow Cubes
- paper and pencils for recording

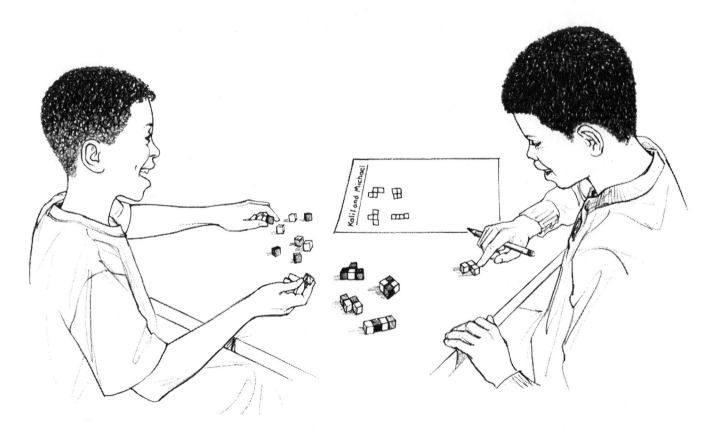

INTRODUCING THE QUESTION

1 **How many different shapes can you make with four Rainbow Cubes?** Have each student build one shape, then ask a volunteer to show the shape she created to the class. Demonstrate that the shapes must be made of cubes with sides in full contact. Turn the shape so students can see it from all angles.

2 Show these two configurations to the class, turning one so that it looks the same as the other. **If you can flip a shape, turn it, or lay it down flat and find it's the same as another shape you've already built, it doesn't count as different.**

3 **First predict how many different shapes you think you'll be able to make. Then make and record as many shapes as you can. Compare your findings with your prediction, and explain how you know you found all the possible shapes.**

WHAT SHOULD YOU DO IF...

▶ Some students have made duplicate shapes?

▶ Some students have difficulty and experience frustration in sketching their shapes?

Some students may not organize their work so that duplicate shapes can be easily seen. **Can you flip, turn, rotate, or lay this shape down flat and make it look like any of your other shapes?**

Recording these shapes will provide a good geometric stretch for your students. Tell them that their sketches do not need to be perfect, but encourage them to persist in their efforts. They may find creative ways of drawing the shapes.

WHAT YOU MIGHT SEE

Some students may not see that these are duplicate shapes.

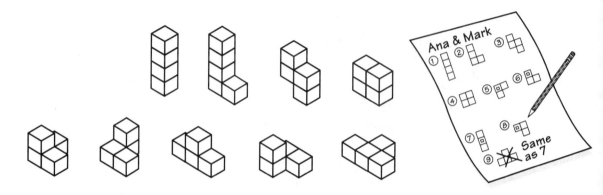

Some students may complete their sketches, think they have found all the shapes, then check and revise their work.

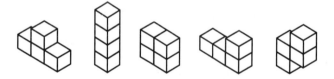

Some students may not readily see the three-dimensional shapes they can build.

WHAT TO LOOK FOR IN STUDENT'S WORK

Was the student able to find many different shapes?

Was the student able to make a prediction?

Was the student able to write about her prediction and her findings?

QUESTIONS FOR DISCUSSION

- How many different shapes did you find?

- Did anyone find a different number of shapes?

- How close was your prediction to your findings? Why do you think so?

- Were you surprised by any of your findings? Why or why not?

- What strategies did you use in looking for duplicate shapes? Explain your thinking.

- Can anyone predict what might happen to the number of shapes possible if the sides of each cube did not have to be in full contact? How do you know?

JOURNAL REFLECTION

Did anything you found out surprise you? Explain.

Write about how you know you could make all the possible shapes.

Predict what might happen to the number of shapes possible if the sides of each cube did not have to be in full contact. How do you know?

Which shape has the greatest perimeter?

Build shapes using 12 Rainbow Cubes. Which shape has the greatest perimeter? Make a recording of your work. Write how you know you found the shape with the greatest perimeter.

MATERIALS

For each pair of students

- Rainbow Cubes
- paper and pencils for recording
- 1-Centimeter Grid Paper (p. 90)

For the overhead projector

- Rainbow Cubes

INTRODUCING THE QUESTION

1 Take out six Rainbow Cubes. Looking at the top of your cubes, what different shapes can you make? There is one rule to follow. The sides of your cubes must be in full contact.

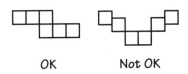

OK   Not OK

On the overhead projector, show several shapes that meet the rule and several that do not.

2 **With your partner, make a shape using six Rainbow Cubes.** Have pairs share their shapes with the class. Leave one pair's shape on the overhead. **What is the perimeter of this shape? How do you know?** Discuss the different strategies students used for finding the perimeter.

3 Now work with your partner to build all the different shapes you can using 12 Rainbow Cubes. Which shape has the greatest perimeter? Make a recording that shows your shapes and their perimeters. Write how you know you found the one with the greatest perimeter.

WHAT SHOULD YOU DO IF...

▶ Some students incorrectly count each cube to come up with the perimeter?

These students may not understand how to find the perimeter. Review with students that to find the perimeter, they should count the units around the outside edge of the shape. **How would you find the perimeter of this shape?**

▶ Some students only see a few different possible shapes?

Some students may only see a few possibilities because they are only making rectangles. As the class is working, you may want to ask the class if anyone has made a shape other than a rectangle. Other students will see that there are more possibilities.

Which Shape Has the Greatest Perimeter? 87

WHAT YOU MIGHT SEE

Some students may find a shape with the greatest perimeter by only making rectangles.

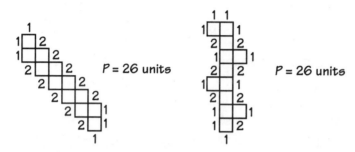

Some students may make shapes other than rectangles.

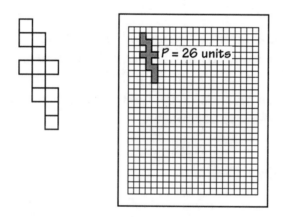

In order to see and count the perimeter more easily, some students may draw their shape on grid paper.

WHAT TO LOOK FOR IN STUDENT'S WORK

Was the student able to make a shape with the greatest perimeter of 26 units?

Was the student able to find the perimeters of her shapes?

Was the student able to make a recording of her shapes and their perimeters?

Was the student able to explain clearly why he was confident he had found one shape with the greatest perimeter?

QUESTIONS FOR DISCUSSION

- How many different shapes were you able to make with 12 cubes?
- Did anyone come up with a different number of shapes?
- How did you go about finding the perimeter of each shape?
- Did anyone do it differently?
- Which shape had the greatest perimeter? What was its perimeter?
- Did anyone find something different?
- What did you find out about shapes and their perimeters?
- What interesting discoveries did you make about perimeter?

JOURNAL REFLECTION

What did you learn about perimeter?

Do different shapes each made with 15 cubes have different perimeters? How do you know?

1-CENTIMETER GRID PAPER

What are all the different numbers?

Use all or some of these Base Ten Blocks:
2 hundreds blocks, 2 tens blocks, 2 ones blocks.
What are all the different numbers you can
represent? Record your work and tell why you
think you have found all the different numbers.

MATERIALS

For each pair of students

- Base Ten Blocks
- paper and pencils for recording

For the overhead projector

- Base Ten Blocks

INTRODUCING THE QUESTION

1 On the overhead projector, show 1 tens block and 2 ones blocks. **If you use all or some of these Base Ten Blocks, what different numbers can you represent? Work with your partner to find how many different numbers you can show using all or some of these blocks.** Allow students a few minutes to work with their partners.

2 **What different numbers can you represent using all or some of these blocks?** (1, 2, 10, 11, 12) Ask several students to share what they found. As they do, show their combinations on the overhead projector. **Do you think that we have found all the possible combinations using just these blocks? How do you know?** Have a brief class discussion so that students can share their thinking.

3 Introduce the question. **Use all or some of these Base Ten Blocks: 2 hundreds blocks, 2 tens blocks, 2 ones blocks. What are all the different numbers you can represent? Record your work and tell why you think you have found all the different numbers.**

WHAT SHOULD YOU DO IF . . .

▶ Some students find 2 or 3 numbers and then stop?

▶ Some students find many, but not all, the possible numbers?

Encourage these students to look for more numbers. **Can you use more or fewer blocks and come up with a different number?**

Some students may have difficulty organizing their work. **How do you know you have found all the different numbers? How could you organize your work so that you know which numbers you already have and which numbers you can still make?**

WHAT YOU MIGHT SEE

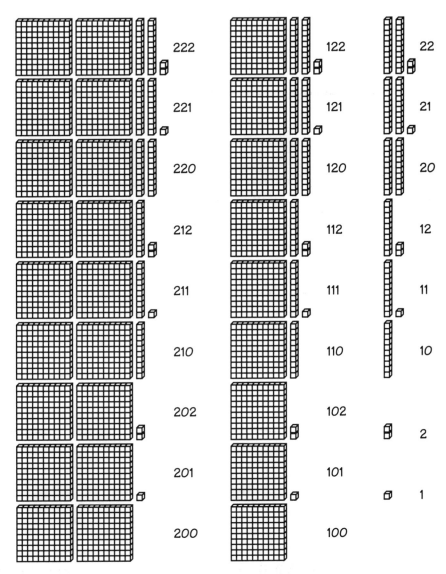

222	122	22
221	121	21
220	120	20
212	112	12
211	111	11
210	110	10
202	102	2
201	101	1
200	100	

Some students may use patterns to find all 26 different numbers.

WHAT TO LOOK FOR IN STUDENT'S WORK

Was the student able to find all 26 different numbers?

Was the student able to determine whether or not she had found all the different numbers?

Does the student's recording clearly explain how she knows she found all the different numbers?

QUESTIONS FOR DISCUSSION

- How many different numbers did you find? What numbers did you find?

- Did anyone find something different? What did you find?

- Do you think you found all the different numbers? How do you know for sure?

- How were you sure you didn't make the same number more than once?

- Did anyone use a different method? What did you do?

- If you were going to work this problem again, would you organize your work differently? How would you do it?

JOURNAL REFLECTION

Could 134 be a number represented by the blocks you worked with on this problem? Explain why or why not.

How would the answer change if you used 1 hundreds block, 3 tens blocks, and 2 ones blocks?

How would adding a thousands block change your work? Explain your thinking.

What could the missing dimensions be?

If a rectangular prism has a volume of 12 cm³ and a length of 2 cm, what could the width and the height be? Use your Base Ten Blocks to help find the width and the height. Make a recording and explain how you know what the missing dimensions could be.

MATERIALS

For each pair of students
- Base Ten Blocks
- paper and pencils for recording

INTRODUCING THE QUESTION

1 **What is a rectangular solid?** Discuss the box-like characteristics of a rectangular solid and have students build a rectangular solid using their Base Ten Blocks.

2 Write the terms *length, width, height,* and *volume* on the chalkboard and discuss their meanings. **How can you measure the width of the solid you built? How can you find the volume?** Have students explain their thinking.

3 Introduce the question. **If a rectangular prism has a volume of 12 cm³ and a length of 2 cm, what could the width and the height be? Make a recording and explain how you know what the missing dimensions could be.**

WHAT SHOULD YOU DO IF . . .

▶ Some students start building shapes that are not rectangular prisms?

Have the students explain to you what they are doing. They may have a slightly different interpretation of the question. **What shape are you building? What does the question ask?**

▶ Some students find the solution quickly?

These students may want to create volume puzzles for classmates to solve. **Try a shape that has a volume of 27 cm³. Make a volume puzzle and include its solution. Trade your puzzle with another student.**

WHAT YOU MIGHT SEE

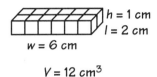

$V = 12\ cm^3$

Some students may find the dimensions for one rectangular prism but may orient it differently in their recording.

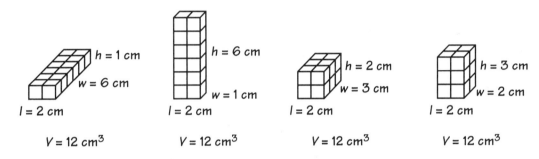

Some students may find all 4 possible solutions.

WHAT TO LOOK FOR IN STUDENT'S WORK

Was the student able to find at least one solution for the width and the height?

Did the student explain how she found the missing dimensions?

Does the student's work reflect an understanding of volume?

QUESTIONS FOR DISCUSSION

- If a rectangular prism has a volume of 12 cm³ and a length of 2 cm, what could the width and the height be? How did you figure it out?

- Who found another possibility? Tell about it. How did you find your solution?

- Do you think there might be another solution? Why or why not?

- Did using your Base Ten Blocks help you solve this question? Why or why not?

- If the width and the length were the same measure, what would the height be? How do you know?

JOURNAL REFLECTION

Think of another way, besides using blocks, that you could teach a younger student that the same volume can have different dimensions.

Suppose you know that the volume of a rectangular prism is 12 cm³. What are all the possibilities for its length, width, and height? How do you know?

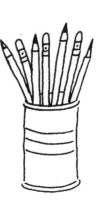

What is the measure of each angle?

Look at the angles of the Pattern Block shapes. What is the measure of each angle in each of the different blocks? Make a recording that gives the measure of each angle. Explain how you know the measures are correct.

MATERIALS

For each pair of students

- Pattern Blocks
- paper, pencils, and crayons for recording

For the overhead projector

- Pattern Blocks

INTRODUCING THE QUESTION

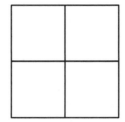

1 Today you are going to calculate the number of degrees in each angle of the Pattern Block shapes without using a protractor. One possible way is to make a complete 360° using like angles of identical blocks. Put a dot in the center of the overhead projector and arrange four orange squares around the dot. **How can you find the number of degrees in one of these angles?** (divide 360° by 4) **What is the measure of one of the angles?** (90°) **Are all of the angles identical?** (yes)

2 Have students work in pairs with their Pattern Blocks. **What is the measure of each angle in each of your Pattern Blocks? Record the measures of all of the angles. Explain how you know the measures are correct.**

WHAT SHOULD YOU DO IF . . .

▶ Some students use the measurement of a triangle, square, or other shape as a reference point to determine other angle measures?

Any workable method students devise for calculating the measures of the angles is acceptable. A variety of approaches will provide for an interesting class discussion at the end of the lesson.

▶ Some students combine different angles of the same block to make 360°?

This method will work with unlike angles, but students will not be able to divide 360° by the number of angles used. Encourage students to check their work if they used unlike angles. **How did you find the measures of these angles? How can you be sure of your work?**

WHAT YOU MIGHT SEE

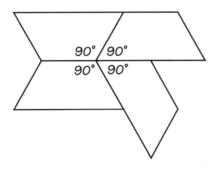

Some students may incorrectly place the Pattern Block shapes around the dot, thus miscalculating the measure of the angle.

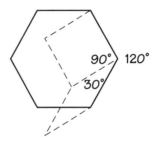

Some students may use angles of Pattern Blocks they have already calculated to assist them in calculating other angle measures.

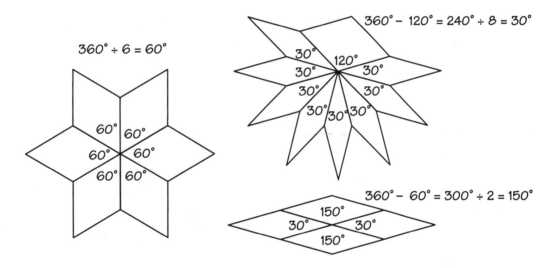

$360° \div 6 = 60°$

$360° - 120° = 240° \div 8 = 30°$

$360° - 60° = 300° \div 2 = 150°$

Some students may correctly find the measure of like angles by orienting the Pattern Block shapes around a dot to make a complete 360°, then dividing by the number of blocks used. Students will have to alter this method slightly when finding the measure of angles in the tan rhombus.

WHAT TO LOOK FOR IN STUDENT'S WORK

Did the student determine the correct measures for each angle in the set of Pattern Block shapes?

Does the student's recording give a clear explanation of how he knows the measures are correct? Is the method he used to calculate the measures a valid one?

QUESTIONS FOR DISCUSSION

- What are the measures of the angles in the Pattern Blocks? Are all the angles within each shape the same? How do you know?

- How did you calculate the measure of the angles? Did anyone use a different method? Were there any shapes that were tricky or more challenging? Why or why not?

- How did you find the measure of the trapezoid and rhombus angles? Did you use a different strategy? What was it?

- Did you find any instance when the "360° method" didn't work? Why was that? How did you measure the angles of the tan rhombus?

JOURNAL REFLECTION

Use four different Pattern Block shapes to create a design. Calculate the total measure of the different angles in the shape. Include a drawing of the design, and label the measure of each angle. Explain how you calculated the total measure.

Find the total value of the angle measures in your set of Pattern Blocks. Explain how you calculated the total.

Constructing Ideas

Number Hunt

CAN WE FIND THINGS IN THE CLASSROOM THAT COME IN GROUPS OF 1 TO 20?

The classroom environment becomes the scene of an ambitious number hunt as students search for groups of 1 to 20 objects. The discoverer of each number group re-creates it as an illustrated counting-book page. Amidst all the fun, students reinforce their estimating and counting skills in a unique and challenging way.

MATERIALS

For each student

❏ full sheets of paper
❏ yarn or staples (for binding book pages together)

PREPARATION

o Gather several counting books from your school or public library.
o Copy the student instructions, page 106, for each student.

STARTING OUT TOGETHER

Take time to read some of the library books aloud. Initiate a conversation with the students about the books you've just shared with them. Ask questions such as the following:

❑ *What did you enjoy most about each book?*

❑ *How are the books alike? How are they different?*

❑ *What is the theme of each book? What's being counted?*

❑ *What do you notice about the pictures in each book? How do the pictures help?*

❑ *How do the illustrations and the numbers in each book go together?*

❑ *What numbers are found in each different book?*

❑ *Do you notice any number or counting patterns in any of the books we read?*

Tell the students that they will be making counting books of their own. Pass out the student instructions (page 104), and read through them with the students Then let the number hunt begin!

Home Work

At home, the students work with their families to make "At Our Home" counting books.

See At Our Home, page 110.

3 busy bees buzzing around the hive.

4 little otters make a slippery slide.

As you talk with individual students, you will find that some are very methodical, looking for their numbers in order, and others are more focused on counting groups of interest to them or things they would particularly like to draw. Let the students take their own approaches to the number hunt, as long as they keep in mind that the end goal is to produce a completed counting book. If the class has difficulty finding groups in the classroom for some numbers, a student who finds a number that has been especially elusive can give a few clues to assist the rest of the class in their search.

Number Hunt

- ❏ Find something in the classroom that comes in a group.
- ❏ Count how many are in the group.
- ❏ Make a page telling the number in the group.
- ❏ Draw a picture of the whole group.
- ❏ Make one page for each number from 1 to 20.

WHILE THE STUDENTS ARE WORKING

Talk with individual students as they go about their number hunt. Ask questions such as the following:

- ❑ *What numbers have you found in your hunt so far?*
- ❑ *What's the next number you'll be searching for?*
- ❑ *How are you deciding what order to search in?*
- ❑ *Are there any numbers you're having trouble finding?*
- ❑ *How many numbers have you made pages for?*
- ❑ *How many more pages do you need to make?*
- ❑ *What numbers (pages) go between these two? How do you know?*

When students have completed a page for each number, they can assemble their pages into a book. They should order their pages from 1 to 20 and bind them together with yarn or staples.

REFLECTING TOGETHER

Before getting together as a class, you might want to have groups of four share their completed, bound counting books. The students in the foursome can either read their books to the others or pass the books around for the others to read and look over individually.

When the groups have had enough time sharing their books together, call the large group back together. Focus the attention of the class on various aspects of their counting books by asking questions such as the following:

- ❑ *Which number did you think was hardest to find? What did some of you find for that number?*
- ❑ *Who made a page for the number 9? What did you show?*
- ❑ *Which numbers were really easy to find? How many different things did we find for some of those numbers?*
- ❑ *Did anyone draw something for the number one that you think no one else did? What was it?*
- ❑ *Do any of you think you have a page that no one else has?*

• • • • • • • • • • • • •
The students will, understandably, be very proud of their completed books. Emphasize what a nice job everyone did. You may want to feature the counting books in your reading corner for a week or so, to allow the students more time to enjoy them. Your students could share the books with other classrooms by sending them around the school as a traveling exhibit.

THE WORK STUDENTS DO

Making their own counting books gives students a chance to really personalize their math work with illustrations and ideas for counting that are all their own. And through the experience of looking for objects in their own classroom environment to count, students are encouraged to see the ways in which math is present in the world around them. Long after their search for numbers in the classroom environment is ended, students will be finding new ways of seeing mathematics in their world.

This student didn't have to look very far to find number one. He started with a self-portrait, making himself number one.

Six PePil Siting ut the Round tabile.

The same student selected his two teachers as the subject of his counting book page for number 2.

Another people-oriented, rather than object-oriented, selection shows a very creative drawing solution to the difficult task of picturing so many students seated around a table. Although the students were not told exactly how to label their pages, this student chose to describe the group in words, as well as showing the numeral, 6.

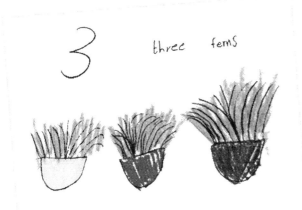

Here is another example in which a student chose to show both the numeral, 3, and the words, "three ferns." The voluntary inclusion of number names on students' pages may be a reflection of how comfortable and confident they are about their ability to write them.

Finding the larger numbers can prove to be a more challenging task. The resourceful student who produced these two counting book pages counted stripes on a pumpkin and parts on a rocking chair.

This student became so immersed in the drawing process that the numeral didn't quite make it onto the page. Unlike commercially produced books, these counting books can be "touched up" or refined even after they are bound if students notice something is missing. The idea of revising work is one that should be encouraged.

Dear Family,

The children have been making posters that show several different designs using the same number of blocks and including one "trick" design showing a different number. The class tries to find the design that has the wrong number of blocks.

Puzzling Picture

Say a number from 3 to 9, and have your child draw a picture showing several groups of that many things, including one group of a different number. For example, for the number 6, your child could draw a picture showing 6 houses, 6 trees, 6 flowers, but 5 people. Send the pictures back to school so that the class can find the "trick design."

The Great Addition Chart

WHAT PATTERNS CAN WE FIND IN THE ADDITION CHART?

As students arrange equations they write for the basic addition facts on a giant wall chart, they begin to look for patterns and to think about ways the equations relate to each other.

....

MATERIALS

For each pair
- ❏ 40 LinkerCubes in 2 colors (20 of each color)
- ❏ 1-cm grid paper, page 90
- ❏ half sheets of paper
- ❏ scissors

PREPARATION

- o Draw a grid on a 3' x 7' piece of butcher paper with spaces that are 3" by 8". Write in the numbers 0−9 to label the rows and columns. (See completed chart, page 115.)
- o Copy the student instructions, page 113, for each pair.
- o Copy the Addition Chart, page 118, for each student.

		4 + 7 = 11	4 + 8 = 12	
5 + 6 = 11		5 + 8 = 13		
6 + 6 = 12	6 + 7 = 13			
8 + 6 = 14			8 + 9 = 17	
		9 + 8 = 17		

STARTING OUT TOGETHER

Show the class a stick of two colors of LinkerCubes, with cubes of the same color together. *I am thinking of an addition equation that tells about these cubes. Who can say the equation?*

Now everyone make a stick with cubes. Think of the addition equation that tells about your cubes. Ask one student to show the class her stick of cubes and say the addition equation that tells about them. *Does anyone else have cubes that show that equation?* Have everyone with a matching stick of cubes stand up.

Have several students say their equations and ask those with sticks of cubes that show the same equation to stand up.

Look together at the addition chart frame you have prepared. *Let's find places for some of the equations you have shown with your cubes. Where do you think 2 + 3 might go? Why would it go there?* The stick of cubes can be temporarily supported on the chart by push pins. Let several students locate where their cubes go on the chart.

Read through the student instructions (page 111) with the class, and have the students work to fill up the chart with grid paper recordings.

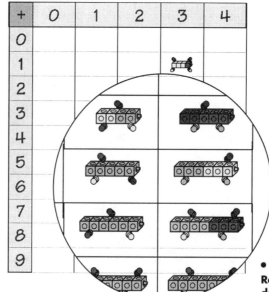

Home Work
Students will look around their homes for objects about which to write addition equations.
See Equations from Home, page 117.

Rather than telling the students to restrict their addends to numbers less than 10, allow them to find out for themselves that there are not spaces on the chart for these equations. Put any "too big" equations students record around the outside of the chart. Some students will take special interest in making these kinds of equations. Don't discourage them.

The Great Addition Chart

- [ ] Use your cubes to show an addition equation.
- [ ] Cut out and color squares on grid paper to match your cubes.
- [ ] Tape the grid paper on the chart. Write the equation it shows.
- [ ] Show other equations with cubes. Make a recording for each equation and put it on the chart.

WHILE THE STUDENTS ARE WORKING

Help the students find the appropriate place on the chart for each recording and write the equation below it. After placing a recording on the chart, a student should begin work on another one. Duplicates of equations already on the chart can be placed one on top of the other.

When students bring recordings to put on the chart, say,

- ❏ *Tell the equation that goes with your recording.*
- ❏ *What if there was one more red cube?*
- ❏ *What would the equation be? How do you know?*

For a short time, students may create equations randomly, making sticks of cubes that appeal to them. After a day or two, some students will begin to look for spaces on the chart where equations are missing and draw recordings for those spaces, often without using the cubes. By allowing students to make this transition naturally, you can have the opportunity to make useful assessment observations.

REFLECTING TOGETHER

Take time to admire the completed chart.

- ❏ *Did you think we could write so many addition equations?*
- ❏ *How many do you think we wrote?*
- ❏ *Do you see any patterns in the chart?*
- ❏ *Do you see any patterns in the rows?*
- ❏ *Do you see any patterns in the columns?*
- ❏ *Where are the doubles facts?*
- ❏ *Some of these facts can be called fact friends because they are alike in some way. Can you find some fact friends on the chart?*

Give each student a copy of the blank Addition Chart you have prepared. Tell students to pick their favorite portion of the chart and copy the equations onto their own addition chart. Talk with students about their reasons for choosing a particular row or rows as their favorites.

• • • • • • • • • • • •
To a student who is able to see mathematics as a network of relationships, facts and operations make a lot more sense. Seen in this context, a "new" problem such as "8 + 7" doesn't seem so brand new at all because the sum can be thought of as simply one more than the "cinchy" fact 7 + 7 = 14.

5 + 5 = 10 will go in that empty space.

THE WORK STUDENTS DO

The mathematical experiences offered in these activities allow students to interact and build meaning at many levels. Students who are allowed this type of control over their learning take that responsibility seriously. Rather than settling for doing the least amount of work or thinking possible, students push themselves to show off their strengths.

Students have a real knack for challenging themselves at the most appropriate levels. The students who produced the work shown on page 114, when asked to copy their favorite equations from the class's Great Addition Chart, responded in a variety of ways, at levels appropriate to their unique abilities.

+	0	1	2	3	4	5	6	7	8	9
0	0 + 0 = 0	0 + 1 = 1	0 + 2		4 = 4	0 + 5 = 5	0 + 6 = 6	0 + 7 = 7	0 + 8 = 8	0 + 9 = 9
1	1 + 0 = 1	1 + 1 =	2 + 2 = 4	2 + 3 = 5		5 = 6	1 + 6 = 7	1 + 7 = 8	1 + 8 = 9	1 + 9 = 10
2	2 + 0 = 2						2 + 6 = 8	2 + 7 = 9	2 + 8 = 10	2 + 9 = 11
3	3 + 0 = 3		3 + 2 = 5	3 + 3 = 6	3		3 + 6 = 9	3 + 7 = 10	3 + 8 = 11	3 + 9 = 12
4	4 + 0 =						+ 6 = 10	4 + 7 = 11	4 + 8 = 12	4 + 9 = 13
5	5 + 0 =		4 + 2 = 6	4 + 3 = 7	4 +		+ 6 = 11	5 + 7 = 12	5 + 8 = 13	5 + 9 = 14
6	6 + 0 =						+ 6 = 12	6 + 7 = 13	6 + 8 = 14	6 + 9 = 15
7	7 + 0 = 7		5 + 2 = 7	5 + 3 = 8			7 + 6 = 13	7 + 7 = 14	7 + 8 = 15	7 + 9 = 16
8	8 + 0 = 8				13		8 + 6 = 14	8 + 7 = 15	8 + 8 = 16	8 + 9 = 17
9	9 + 0 = 9	9 + 1 =			+ 5 = 14		9 + 6 = 15	9 + 7 = 16	9 + 8 = 17	9 + 9 = 18

The mechanical aspects of writing are still a great challenge to this student. She felt a sense of accomplishment at having completed this portion of the Addition Chart.

This child, like many others in her class, decided she'd like to make her own copy of the entire Addition Chart.

Expanding on some of the discussions the class had had about the Addition Chart and its many patterns, this student decided not only to reproduce the entire chart, but to color code the patterns he found as well. He even included a key to his color code on the back of his paper!

Date _____

Dear Family,

This week the class is discovering how numbers are made up of smaller numbers. It is obvious to an adult that 5 can be seen as 2 and 3, but to a young child this is new learning.

The Two Hands Game I

Play the game below several times with your child, selecting a different number of counters each day.

- ❑ Start with 5 small objects, such as pennies or beans. Secretly close your two hands with some in each saying, "5 is…"
- ❑ Open first one hand, then the other, saying for example, "2… and 3."
- ❑ Repeat the game many times, encouraging your child to chant along with you.
- ❑ Switch roles, letting your child hold the counters.

6 chairs in the kitchen and 4 chairs in the family room. That's 10 chairs all together. 6 + 4 = 10.

+	0	1	2	3	4	5	6	7	8	9
0										
1										
2										
3										
4										
5										
6										
7										
8										
9										

Train Park

WHAT HAPPENS WHEN WE MAKE A LONG PATTERN TRAIN INTO SHORTER TRAINS AND PARK THEM IN SPECIAL WAYS?

The world is full of patterns—patterns inside of patterns, patterns that remind us of other patterns, and patterns that lead to other patterns. As students transform linear cube patterns into two-dimensional patterns, new patterns are revealed. The challenge of recording their patterns continues as they make train park posters.

MATERIALS

For each pair

❏ 100 LinkerCubes in two colors (50 of each color)
❏ 2-cm grid paper, inside back cover page
❏ 12" x 18" construction paper
❏ scissors
❏ paste

PREPARATION

o Use 2-cm grid paper and construction paper to make a poster like the one shown below, coloring the squares yellow and green.
o Copy the student instructions, page 121, for each pair.

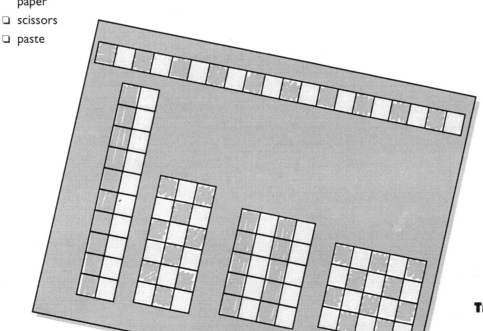

STARTING OUT TOGETHER

Spread out a bag of 100 yellow and green LinkerCubes. Start an ABABAB pattern, such as *snap, clap, snap, clap.* **How could we make a train with cubes to show this pattern? Let's make four trains just alike that show that pattern.** Separate the students into four groups. Have each group use 25 yellow and green LinkerCubes to make a pattern train for the ABABAB pattern.

Using the first group's train, break off a two-cube car, sliding the rest of the train under it, then break off a second two-cube car, and so on.

Talk about the patterns in the two-cube cars that have been parked. **What do you notice about the way the cubes look now? Do you see any patterns? What name could we give this pattern?**

Ask students to predict what will happen when you break the second group's train into three-cube cars. Choose someone to break the train into three-cube cars, each parked below the other. Discuss the resulting checkered pattern. Then break apart the third group's train into four-cube cars and the fourth group's train into five-cube cars, parking the cars as before.

 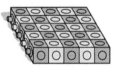

Show the recording you made (see Preparation, page 44). **This recording tells about the pattern train. Why do you think the recording is made like this? What do the different parts tell?**

Read through the student instructions, page 119, with the class and have the students work in pairs to make their own train park patterns and posters.

Home Work

At home, the students will be coloring patterns on grid paper. Send home several sheets of 2-cm grid paper. See Patterns of Squares, page 125.

• • • • • • • • • • • • •
When children are excited about what they are learning, their enthusiasm is naturally carried home with them. One girl who finished her poster for Train Park earlier than the rest of the class went home that night and asked her little brother (a kindergartner) to create a pattern for her to use to make another poster. He drew an ABAB pattern. She brought it to school the next day and together with her partner created a Train Park poster for her brother's pattern.

Train Park

Use your cubes to make four long trains in the same pattern. Color grid paper to match the pattern of your long trains. Fold your construction paper about 2 inches from one long edge. Paste the grid paper above the fold.

1. Break apart one train into cars that have two cubes. Park the cars under each other.
2. Break apart one train into cars that have three cubes. Park the cars under each other.
3. Break apart one train into cars that have four cubes. Park the cars under each other.
4. Break apart one train into cars that have five cubes. Park the cars under each other.

Color grid paper to match each train park.

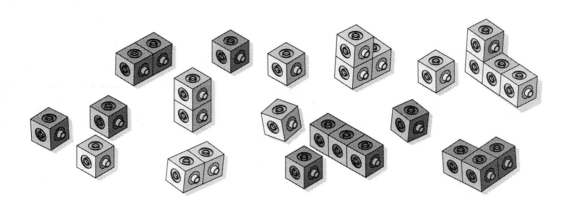

WHILE THE STUDENTS ARE WORKING

You might want to have all the students work on the same patterns. Ask students to suggest patterns the class might work on. Write their ideas on the chalkboard, using colored chalk to write the color names.

At first, the students may need you to demonstrate again or provide individual help for them to get started breaking apart each of their four trains in a different way (two-cube cars, three-cube cars, four-cube cars, and five-cube cars) and parking the cars. Sit with pairs of students as they work on this activity. Ask individuals:

❑ *What do you think will happen when you break this train into twos? (into threes? fours? fives?)*

❑ *What do you notice about the poster you just finished? Describe the patterns you see.*

❑ *What was tricky about making these patterns?*

❑ *What pattern will you try next?*

The construction paper on which students record their train park patterns needs to be folded down about two inches from the top. Students should paste their original long train recording above the fold so that it can be folded back and hidden for the Reflecting Together activity. They should paste the other train recordings below the fold and write words, letters or numbers to tell about the patterns.

REFLECTING TOGETHER

Have each pair bring their favorite poster to the rug. The students should sit in a semicircle so they all are facing the same way. Display the posters so everyone can see them.

Ask questions such as the following:

❑ *What are some things you notice about our posters?*

❑ *Who can tell about their poster and how they made it?*

❑ *What are some ways we could describe these patterns?*

❑ *Do you see any patterns that are alike? How are they alike?*

❑ *What surprised you about the patterns?*

Put all of the posters in a stack. Hold up one poster, folding back the strip at the top that shows the long pattern. **Let's read each one of these break-apart designs. For the first design, we'll read the pattern by saying the color words.** Read each row of the pattern, left to right. Ask the students to predict the pattern of the long train, which you have hidden by folding back the strip at the top. They should tell the reasoning behind their predictions. Then fold up the top of the poster to reveal the long train and read its pattern. Do this with other trains.

Reading the break-apart patterns on the posters presents a new challenge: finding the pattern and its rhythm in recordings that are broken into rows. To predict that the pattern of the hidden long train is the same as the pattern of its parked cars, the students must recall the procedure by which they broke apart the long train to park the cars and reverse their thinking. Mental flexibility is encouraged through this kind of thinking.

THE WORK STUDENTS DO

The quantities of work produced by each pair of students will differ. Some will find the recording to be difficult and time-consuming. To guide the students, suggest that they begin with simple patterns and increase the complexity of the patterns if they feel confident and have time. Although learning to record is an important aspect of the activity, some students could be given the option of not recording after they have completed at least one recording if it slows the pace too much for them. Their work could be photographed to share with the teacher or a classmate instead.

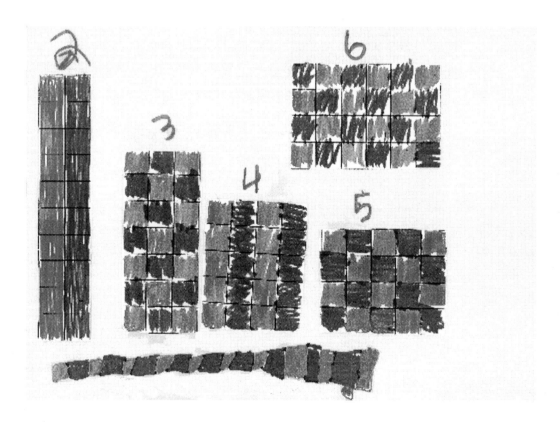

It is important to allow plenty of time for the students to discuss the work produced by the class as a whole. By taking the time to display the posters so that students can discuss things they notice in one another's posters, the potential opportunities for learning go beyond the individuals' experiences with their own work.

Dear Family,

Our class has been busy thinking about patterns and connecting cubes to make trains, each with its own special pattern. It's fun to figure out the patterns and build a train of colored cubes to match.

Tap, Clap

Try some sound patterns at home with your child. You start the pattern, with your child joining in after catching on to it. Here are some patterns to try:

- ❏ Tap, clap, tap, clap, tap, clap …
- ❏ Clap, clap, tap, clap, clap, tap…
- ❏ Tap, tap, clap, clap, tap, tap, clap, clap…

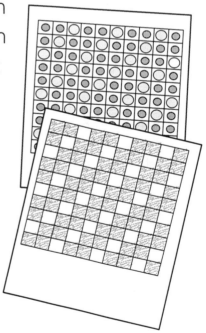

Fraction Folding

HOW CAN WE FOLD A RECTANGULAR SHEET OF PAPER INTO FIFTHS?

Fraction Folding will give your students an opportunity to become familiar with their fraction pieces and to begin to construct mental pictures of halves, thirds, fourths, fifths, sixths, eighths, tenths, and twelfths.

· ·

MATERIALS

For each pair

❑ Fraction Circles PLUS™ or Fraction Builder™
❑ scratch paper
❑ chart paper
❑ colored construction paper
❑ glue sticks
❑ scissors
❑ envelopes (for students to store their cut-out fractions before gluing)
❑ full sheets of paper

PREPARATION

o Make a copy of the student instructions, page 128, for each pair.
o If you choose to do Part 2 of this exploration, you will need to prepare eight sheets of chart paper, each with a fraction title such as Halves, Thirds, Fourths, and so on. Post the chart paper around the room. See the illustration on page 130.

STARTING OUT TOGETHER

PART 1

For the next few days, you and your partner will be making posters to show the same fractions that are in the fraction sets. Decide with your partner whether to use wholes that are circles or wholes that are rectangles for your first fraction poster.

Have students find rectangular or circular objects in the room to trace. They should trace and cut out at least eight copies of the shape from scratch paper. They should fold and cut the scratch paper shapes to show the various fractions. When satisfied with their paper versions of each fraction, the students should trace and cut them out of colored construction paper, label them, and glue them onto chart paper to make a poster. When the students have finished their first poster, encourage them to make another with the alternative shape.

When the students have finished their posters, ask them to write about some ways they learned to show fractions by folding.

PART 2

On a different day you may want to continue this investigation by asking students to think of as many different ways as they can to show fractional parts with squares. **How many ways can you find for halves? How about thirds? Tenths?** When students find new examples, they should color to show the fractional parts.

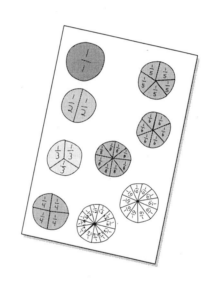

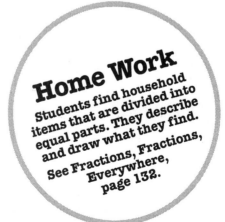

Home Work
Students find household items that are divided into equal parts. They describe and draw what they find. See Fractions, Fractions, Everywhere, page 132.

• • • • • • • • • • •
If you have a 5th or 6th grade class you may want to challenge your students to show the following fractions by folding and shading paper shapes: $\frac{2}{4}$, $\frac{3}{5}$, $\frac{2}{3}$, $\frac{4}{6}$, $\frac{2}{12}$, $\frac{6}{8}$, $\frac{8}{10}$. For example, to show $\frac{2}{3}$ a student would fold her paper shape into thirds and then shade two of the thirds.

Fraction Folding

With your partner:

1. Decide whether to use wholes that are circles or wholes that are rectangles for your first Fraction Folding Poster.

2. Find an item in the classroom that is the shape you and your partner chose. On scratch paper, trace and cut out at least eight copies of the shape.

3. Fold and cut your shapes so that you have one to represent each of the fractions found in your fraction set, (halves, thirds, fourths, fifths, sixths, eighths, tenths, and twelfths).

4. When you are satisfied with your paper fractions, trace and cut them out of colored construction paper.

5. Label your construction paper fraction pieces and glue them onto chart paper to make a poster.

6. When your poster is finished, start another one with a different shape.

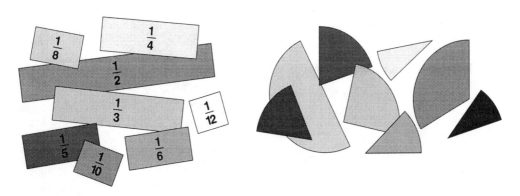

WHILE THE STUDENTS ARE WORKING

As the students work on their fraction folding, take time to ask pairs about their thinking.

❏ *What fractions have you folded so far? Show me how you folded them.*

For Part 2 of the exploration, as students find new examples for each type of fraction, they should display them on the chart paper which you have labeled and posted around the room.

REFLECTING TOGETHER

When the students have finished their first poster, discuss together the students' experiences with folding fractions.

❏ *Which fractions were easy to fold? Which fractions did you have difficulty folding?*

❏ *Did anyone come up with an easier way to fold fractions that were difficult?*

During Part 2 of the exploration, students will find that there are many different ways to divide squares correctly into fractional parts. Most students will focus on ways where the various parts are congruent, that is, exactly the same size and shape. After the students have worked for a while, draw a square divided like the one below on the chalkboard. Ask the class,

❏ *Are these fourths? Why or why not?*

The students will find that choosing a large object to trace results in a very large fraction poster and that, conversely, if they choose a small object for their shapes, tenths and twelfths will be very difficult to tell apart. Let them make these discoveries on their own. Avoid trying to control the activity so that everything works perfectly. It is much more interesting to see the diverse posters which result from this activity than to have students produce posters that look exactly alike.

Folding paper to show fractional parts of shapes encourages thinking about equivalence. A good way to fold sixths is to start by folding halves, then fold the halves into thirds to make sixths. In order to use this strategy, students must think about the relationships between halves and thirds and sixths. It is important to have the students go on to trace a different shape and repeat the paper-folding exploration with the same fractions after the class discussion. This gives them a chance to incorporate the ideas of others into their own strategies. Do not expect all students to perfect these thinking strategies today, however.

THE WORK STUDENTS DO

Fractions can be a difficult concept for some students. Although the concept of fractions is an integral part of our number system, students' well-established ideas about whole numbers are challenged by the introduction of fractions. The simple assumption that 2 is always less than 3 no longer applies when students are comparing $\frac{1}{2}$ to $\frac{1}{3}$. It is important to give students ample opportunity to build on their informal language and to represent the new number concepts in various situations and with manipulatives.

This pair chose to work with a rectangular shape. When asked about their work, they said that the uneven fractions were much trickier to fold than even ones. They agreed that fifths were the hardest.

Fraction Folding gave these students' visual-thinking skills a workout that will help them as they move on to more complex fraction ideas.

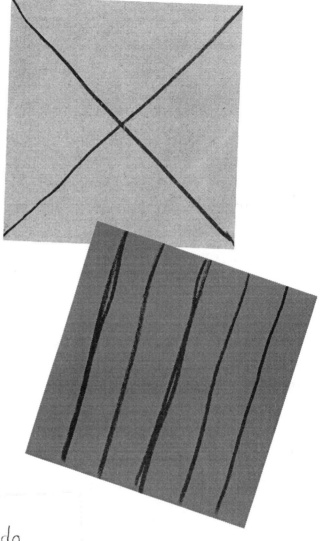

I figured out how to do the 12^ths by folding my paper into 6^ths and then I folded it in half and I had 12^ths because 6 x 2 = 12. for the thirds and fiths by just folding my paper 2 or 4 times.

Having students write about their thinking raises their own awareness of their strategies and thought processes.

Date _____

Dear Student,

This week you have been making fraction pieces by folding and cutting rectangles and circles into equal parts. You have been identifying the fractional parts as halves, thirds, fourths, and so on.

Fractions, Fractions, Everywhere

Look around your home for items that are divided into equal parts. Draw pictures of items you find and name the fractions they show.

Here are some ideas to get you started in your search:

- ❏ panes in windows
- ❏ cabinets in the kitchen
- ❏ sections in an orange
- ❏ seat cushions on the sofa

It All Adds Up

CAN WE CREATE AN EQUATION WITH 6 NUMBERS WHOSE SUM IS ONE MILLION?

It's another millions challenge! This time your students will try to come up with six numbers (a 1-digit, 2-digit, 3-digit, 4-digit, 5-digit, and 6-digit) whose sum comes as close to a million as possible.

MATERIALS

For each pair

❑ calculator
❑ full sheets of paper
❑ scratch paper

PREPARATION

o Make a copy of the student instructions, page 135, for each pair of students.

STARTING OUT TOGETHER

Today I have a challenge for you: Find 6 numbers whose sum is close to one million. The trick is that one number has to have 1 digit, another 2 digits, another 3 digits, and so on, up to 6 digits.

On the chalkboard write the equation 1 + 10 + 100 + 1,000 + 10,000 + 100,000 = 111,111. **This equation follows the rules, but the sum is not very close to one million at all. Work with your partner and use your calculator to come up with 6 numbers to add and see how close you can get to one million.**

Have the students make recordings that show their equation that came closest to a million along with an explanation of the strategies they used.

Home Work
At home students try out a new strategy for finding 6 numbers whose sum is as close to a million as possible. See *Can You Make a Million?*, page 139.

See *Can You Make a Million?*, page 139.

• • • • • • • • • • • • •
Keep in mind that using a variety of approaches and reaching a variety of solutions are the goals of this investigation rather than producing one single "right" answer. What students gain from going through the thinking process and sharing their approaches is much more valuable than getting one exact answer.

It All Adds Up

With your partner:

1. Work to find 6 numbers (a 1-digit, 2-digit, 3-digit, 4-digit, 5-digit, and 6-digit) whose sum comes as close to a million as possible.

2. Use scratch paper and your calculator and work until you have developed an equation whose sum is one million or close to one million.

3. Make a recording that shows your equation whose sum came closest to a million along with an explanation of the strategies you used.

4. Can you think of any other strategies you could use to make more equations?

WHILE THE STUDENTS ARE WORKING

As the students work, visit with various pairs and discuss their thinking.

- ❏ *Tell me about your best equation so far. Show me how it follows the rules.*

- ❏ *Would you say that the sum is close to one million? Could you get it closer?*

- ❏ *What changes are you going to make for your next try?*

REFLECTING TOGETHER

At the end of math time, have pairs share some of their equations.

- ❏ *Tell us about your equation. What strategies did you use?*

- ❏ *What changes did you make when the equations you tried were not close to a million?*

- ❏ *Did anyone use a different strategy? Tell us about it.*

- ❏ *How did you and your partner work together on the equation?*

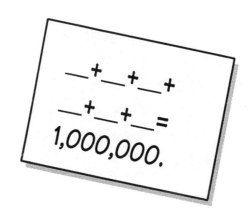

• • • • • • • • • • • • • •

To lessen competition over getting the "closest to one million equation," have students volunteer equations in several other categories as well. Some possible categories are: farthest from one million, most interesting, best pattern, and most unusual. Let the class select some of these equations to add to your bulletin board under the heading "Equations that Come Close to One Million."

THE WORK STUDENTS DO

Throughout *Constructing Ideas About Large Numbers* students are encouraged to use logical thinking to create personal strategies for solving mathematical problems. Because individuals are allowed to think about problems in ways that are logical to them, students at a variety of different mathematical levels can approach and experience success with problems. Having a personal investment and understanding of their solution processes also keeps the students connected to the meaning of their answers.

In It All Adds Up students were asked to find 6 numbers whose sum is close to one million. The work below shows diversity not only in the approaches different students took to the problem, but in the levels of their mathematical thinking.

This pair solved the problem with a guess, check, and adjust strategy. This strategy may not have been as quick as some of the other methods, but it worked for and made sense to these students.

912253
84411
3211
112
12
+
1000000 = 1000000

We kept adding up numbers and each time we changed them a little. It was pretty hard. It took a long time but we finally did it. We kept getting close then we'd say oh no and try some more. so they finally made 1,000,000. My partner found a quicker way after we were done but we like this way best.

98764 8 - not enough → 1,000,000

What we did is we added up 5s
like 5+55+555 then we could see
we needed more so we tried more
numbers. 8s weren't enough, 9s
were too much. So we used 8s
and saw which ones we had
to make 9s. We kept changing
to 9s. We got 999998. We
changed 2 more to nine
and we had a million!!!

This pair took the guess, check, and adjust strategy one step further. They started with all like-numbers and worked to find which numbers would get their answer closest to a million. They decided eights were as close as they could get. Then they worked with the difference between their sum and a million, changing eights to nines one at a time and adjusting the sum until they reached one million. Using only two numbers made the problem more approachable for these children.

900,000
90,000
9,000
900
9   8 ← First row
+   2
―――――――
1,000,000

In the First row
you put any # 1-9 in it.
Then in the second row
you put the # that eqcals
10 with that #. Then you put a
Nine in front of every # and
put zeros at the end and it will
equal a million if you add it all up.

973,243
 23,334
  3,202
    210
     10
+   1
―――――――
1,000,000

The Ones Collumn
Must equall 10 and all
the others have to equall
to 9.

These pairs made an amazing discovery! By approaching the problem "backwards", (looking at the answer first then working back to the equation), these students found a "tricky" way to solve the problem. To arrive at one million they found that, "The ones column must equal 10 and all the others have to equal 9."

Date _____

Dear Student,

This week you have been working in groups of four to make Thousand Collections. Each group is gathering, counting, and arranging 1000 items. You are displaying your collections in an organized way so that someone can see that there are 1000 items without having to count every one.

Thousands Hunt

Look around for a group of items that would number more than 1000. It's not important to know the exact number of items there are all together, but you should be able to convince someone that there are more than 1000 items. Some ideas are:

- ❏ letters on a page of the newspaper
- ❏ pages in a dictionary
- ❏ footsteps from home to school
- ❏ stars in the sky
- ❏ drops of water in the bathtub
- ❏ blades of grass in a lawn

Write about the group of item you choose. Tell how you know there are more than 1000. Bring your paper back to school.

What's the Question?

WHAT'S THE QUESTION BEHIND THE PROBLEM?

Instead of being presented a set of rules for solving multiplication and division problems involving fractions, students rely on what they already know to interpret the problems in ways that make sense to them.

....

MATERIALS

For each pair

❑ Fraction Circles PLUS™ (one set of 51 pieces)
❑ full sheets of paper

PREPARATION

o You will need transparent Fraction Circles PLUS™ for the overhead projector.
o Copy the student instructions, page 142, and the Rules for Multiplying and Dividing with Fractions, page 147, for each pair.
o Title chart paper "Problems from Our Class."

STARTING OUT TOGETHER

On the overhead projector, write: 2×4. **When you read the multiplication symbol as "groups of," the question asked by this problem is: What's 2 groups of 4?** Write the question next to the problem. Write several more examples, such as 6×3 and 4×2, and have the students interpret each problem by telling the question it asks.

On the overhead projector, write the problems: $2 \times \frac{1}{4}$, $\frac{1}{2} \times \frac{1}{4}$, and $\frac{1}{4} \times \frac{1}{2}$. **These problems are a little different. Work with your partner to figure out the question asked by each problem and the answer. Use Fraction Circles or draw sketches, if you like.** Give the class time to work, then discuss each problem.

❑ *What question does this problem ask?*

❑ *What answer did you get? Can anyone use the overhead Fraction Circles to show us how they solved the problem?*

❑ *Did anyone get a different answer?*

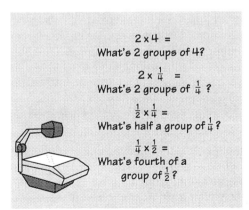

Introduce the language for division problems. On the overhead projector write the problems: $4 \div \frac{1}{2}$; $\frac{1}{2} \div \frac{1}{4}$; $\frac{1}{4} \div \frac{1}{2}$. **Work with your partner to figure out the question asked by each problem and the answer. Record your thinking about each problem and the answer you ended up with.**

After giving the students time to work, regroup and discuss each problem, having the students tell what question it asks, give the answer, and explain it with Fraction Circles on the overhead projector. Then pass out a copy of the student instructions (page 142) to each pair.

Home Work

At home, the students show their parents the method they've been using to solve multiplication and division problems involving fractions.

See Show and Tell, page 146.

• • • • • • • • • • • • • • • •

Rather than relying on algorithms, where memorization of rules is the focus, the approach here relies heavily on active thinking. To solve problems such as , students need to be able to verbalize the question: How many halves are there in one fourth? This kind of fluency enables students to use their own logical and visual thinking skills to really know what the solution (There is one half of in) means in relation to the problem.

What's the Question?

Work with your partner to solve as many of these problems as you can. Use your Fraction Circles or draw sketches to help with your thinking. Keep a **Problems Log** in which you record:

❑ all the problems on which you work

❑ the solution you find for each problem

❑ a sketch or written explanation of each problem

Choose from these problems.

$3 \times \frac{1}{4}$ $\qquad$ $3 \div \frac{1}{2}$

$5 \times \frac{1}{4}$ $\qquad$ $\frac{3}{4} \div \frac{1}{4}$

$\frac{1}{3} \times 12$ $\qquad$ $\frac{1}{2} \div \frac{1}{6}$

$\frac{1}{2} \times 6$ $\qquad$ $\frac{1}{2} \div \frac{2}{8}$

$\frac{1}{2} \times \frac{1}{4}$ $\qquad$ $6\frac{1}{2} \div \frac{1}{4}$

$\frac{1}{3} \times \frac{3}{4}$ $\qquad$ $2 \div \frac{1}{8}$

$\frac{2}{3} \times \frac{3}{4}$ $\qquad$ $\frac{4}{6} \div \frac{1}{6}$

$\frac{1}{3} \times \frac{3}{6}$ $\qquad$ $3 \div \frac{1}{6}$

WHILE THE STUDENTS ARE WORKING

After the pairs have worked for a while, tell them that if they finish solving all the problems on the list you gave them, they can make up some of their own problems for the class to try. *The only rule for adding problems to this list is that you must be able to solve the problem before adding it. Write the problem on the chart paper titled "Problems from Our Class," but keep your own copy of the solution. Let your classmates try to solve the problem for themselves.*

Ask individual pairs questions to see how their work is going.

❑ *Which problems on the list are the easiest for you to solve? Why?*

❑ *Which type of problems are you finding to be the toughest?*

❑ *What are you finding out about multiplication and division of fractions? Are you coming up with any rules of your own about these types of problems?*

❑ *Have you added a problem to our class list?*

❑ *Have you tried to solve any of the problems someone else has added to the class list?*

REFLECTING TOGETHER

Tell the students that the approach they have been using for the multiplication and division of fractions has relied on their own good thinking and number sense. *Today, I'm going to give you a chance to try rules that some people use and see if they give the same solutions to the problems on our list as we found earlier this week.*

Pass out a copy of the Rules for Multiplying and Dividing with Fractions (page 101) to each pair of students. Read through the steps and explain how to use the algorithm to solve these problems:

$$3 \times \frac{1}{5} \qquad \frac{1}{4} \times \frac{1}{3} \qquad \frac{1}{4} \times 12$$

$$4 \div \frac{1}{2} \qquad \frac{5}{6} \div \frac{1}{6} \qquad \frac{1}{2} \div \frac{1}{6}$$

See if the answers you get by using the rules match up with the answers you got for the problems in your Problems Log. Choose one problem that you worked both ways and write about how the two solution methods compare.

Discuss the students' experiences with the standard rules.

❑ *How did these rules work for you?*

❑ *Did using the rules produce the same solutions as your own method?*

❑ *Do the rules make sense with what you already knew about fractions? Why or why not?*

• • • • • • • • • • • • • •

For the Problems from Our Class list, students may create problems such as $\frac{1}{2} \div 6$ and may have difficulty using a question such as "How many sixes are there in $\frac{1}{2}$?" to find the solution. To solve division problems of this type, a more useful way of phrasing the question is, for example: If $\frac{1}{2}$ is divided into 6 pieces, how much is each piece? The ability to read a problem in both ways gives students the flexibility to choose the question that makes the most sense given the context of any particular problem.

THE WORK STUDENTS DO

Some teachers are concerned about what will happen to students' test scores if they are not taught rules for fraction operations. "Won't my students' performance on standardized test scores suffer?" they wonder.

When students are able to think about fractions in the way in which they are asked to think in these explorations, they actually may experience more success on standardized tests than if they were simply to apply rules and algorithms in a rote manner. Students who have a strong understanding of equivalence, can approach new problems logically, and can estimate answers are at an advantage because they are able to quickly rule out multiple-choice test answers that don't make sense.

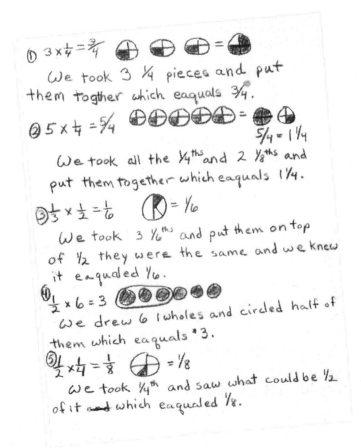

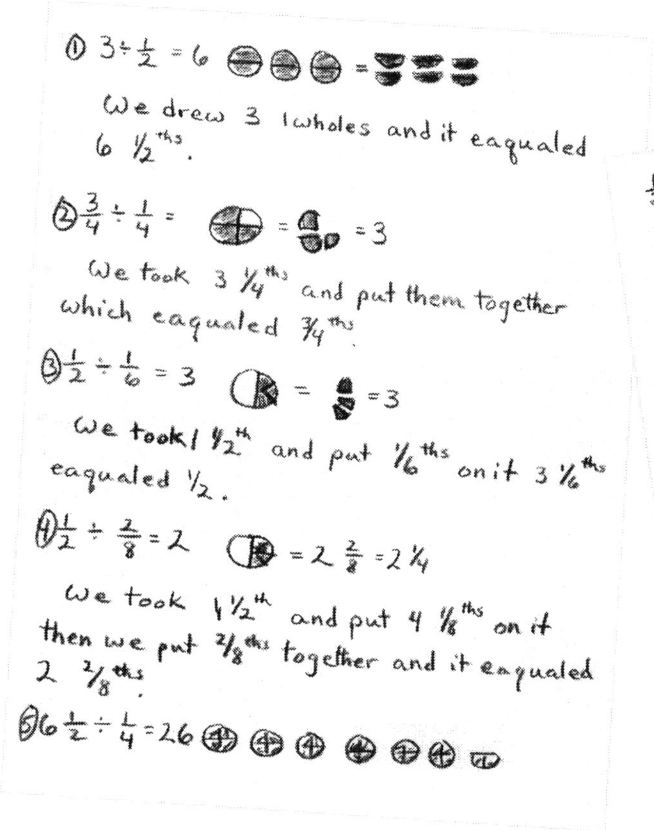

① $3 \div \frac{1}{2} = 6$ ⊖⊘⊘⊘ = ⊖⊖⊖

We drew 3 1wholes and it eaqualed 6 ½ths.

② $\frac{3}{4} \div \frac{1}{4} =$ ⊕ = ⬤ = 3

We took 3 ¼ths and put them together which eaqualed ¾ths.

③ $\frac{1}{2} \div \frac{1}{6} = 3$ ◕ = ⬤ = 3

We took 1 ½th and put ⅙ths on it 3 ⅙ths eaqualed ½.

④ $\frac{1}{2} \div \frac{2}{8} = 2$ ◐ = 2 $\frac{2}{8}$ = 2 ¼

We took 1 ½th and put 4 ⅛ths on it then we put ²⁄₈ths together and it eaqualed 2 ²⁄₈ths.

⑤ $6\frac{1}{2} \div \frac{1}{4} = 26$ ⊕ ⊕ ⊕ ⊕ ⊕ ⊕ ⊖

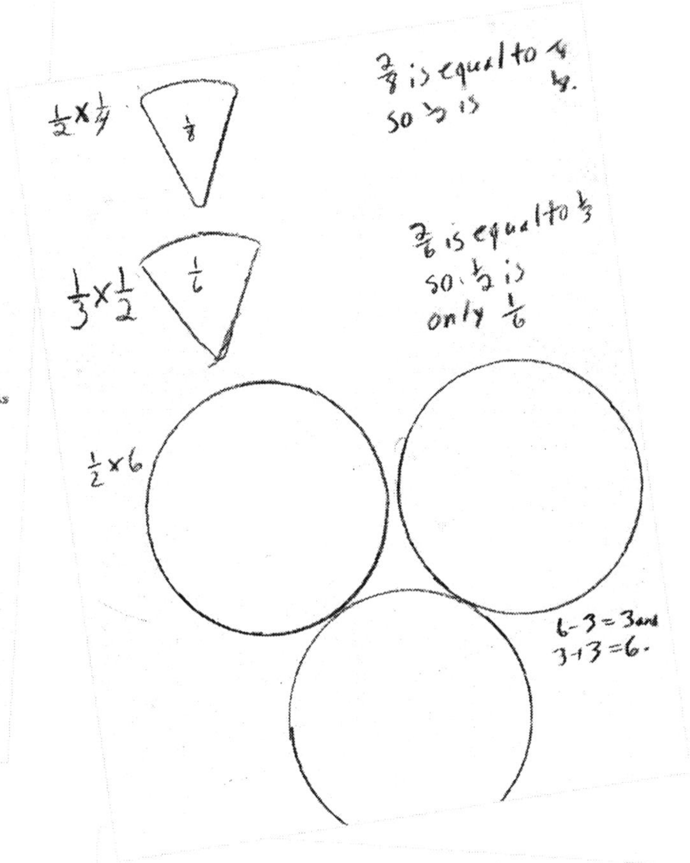

$\frac{1}{2} \times \frac{1}{4}$ △ $\frac{1}{8}$

$\frac{1}{3} \times \frac{1}{2}$ △ $\frac{1}{6}$

$\frac{2}{8}$ is equal to ¼.
so ½ is

$\frac{2}{6}$ is equal to ⅓
so ½ is only ⅙

$\frac{1}{2} \times 6$

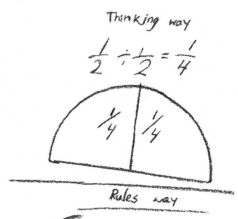

6-3 = 3 and 3+3 = 6.

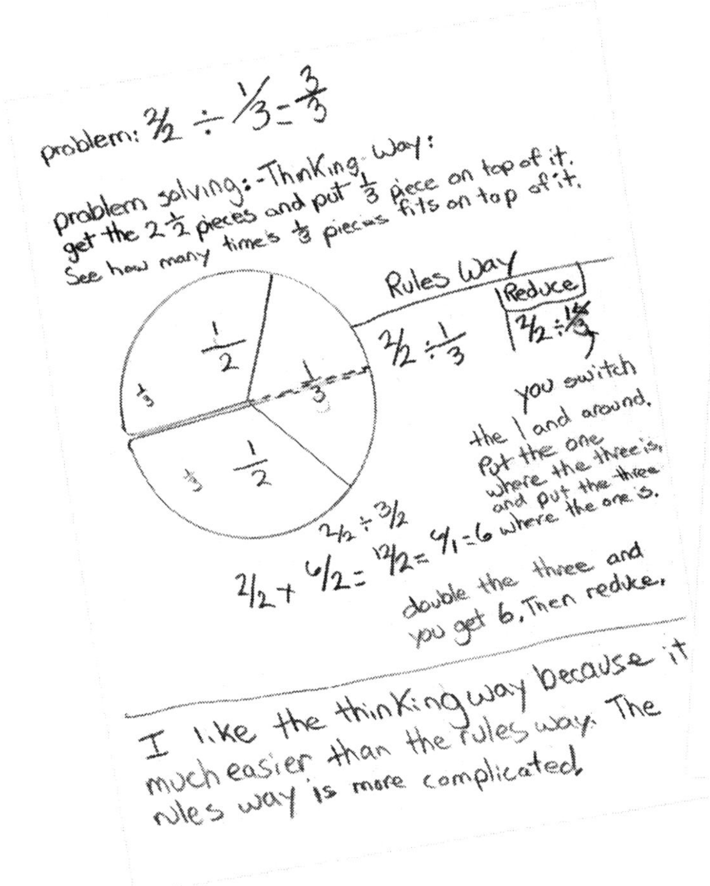

problem: $\frac{2}{2} \div \frac{1}{3} = \frac{3}{3}$

problem solving:-Thinking Way: get the 2 ½ pieces and put ⅓ piece on top of it. See how many times ⅓ pieces fits on top of it.

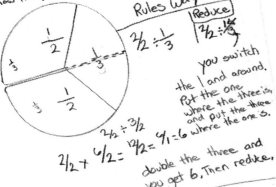

Rules Way | Reduce |
$\frac{2}{2} \div \frac{1}{3}$ $\frac{2}{2} \div \frac{1}{3}$

you switch the 1 and around. Put the one, where the three is, and put the three where the one is.
$\frac{2}{2} \div \frac{3}{2}$
$\frac{2}{2} + \frac{6}{2} = \frac{12}{2} = \frac{6}{1} = 6$
double the three and you get 6. Then reduce.

I like the thinking way because it much easier than the rules way. The rules way is more complicated

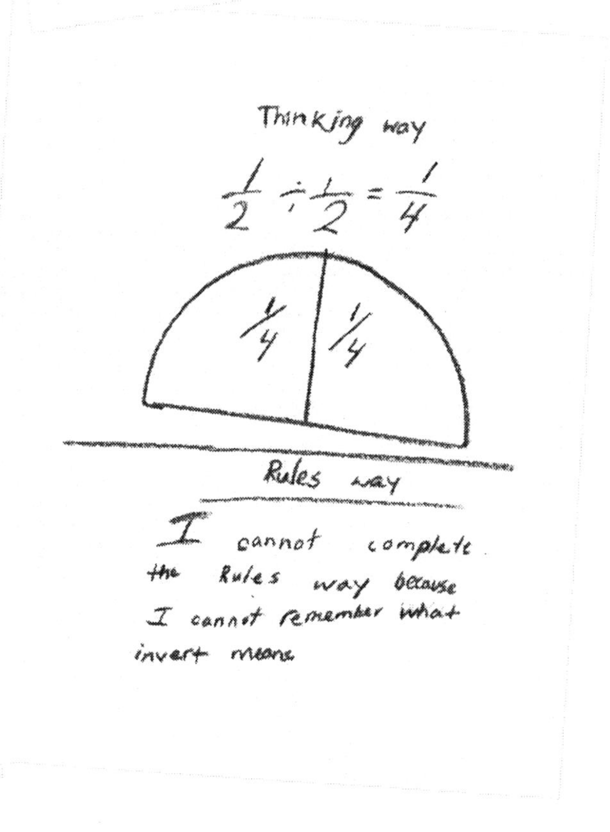

Thinking way

$\frac{1}{2} \div \frac{1}{2} = \frac{1}{4}$

$\frac{1}{4}$ $\frac{1}{4}$

Rules way

I cannot complete the Rules way because I cannot remember what invert means

Dear Student,

You've been thinking about the language of multiplication and division with fractions. You're learning to think about the questions asked by problems such as $\frac{1}{2} \times \frac{1}{2}$ (What's one half of a group of one half?) and $\frac{1}{2} \div \frac{1}{4}$ (How many one fourths are there in one half?).

Show and Tell

Home Work

When adults you know learned to multiply and divide fractions in school, they most likely were taught ways that are very different from the ways you're using this week.

Take some time to think about the problems below.

$2 \times \frac{1}{4}$

$6 \div \frac{1}{2}$

When you are ready, show an adult how you would solve each one. First, tell the question each problem is asking. Then explain how you figured out the answer. Draw sketches to illustrate your solutions.

Ask the adult to explain how he or she would solve each problem. Can the adult explain the reason why his or her method works?

TRUE AND FALSE EQUATION STRIPS

$\dfrac{1}{3} + \dfrac{1}{12} = \dfrac{5}{12}$

$\dfrac{1}{4} + \dfrac{3}{4} = \dfrac{4}{4}$

$\dfrac{3}{9} - \dfrac{1}{3} = 0$

$\dfrac{1}{3} + \dfrac{3}{12} = \dfrac{7}{12}$

$\dfrac{2}{5} + \dfrac{1}{5} = \dfrac{3}{5}$

$\dfrac{1}{3} + \dfrac{2}{3} = 1$

$\dfrac{1}{2} + \dfrac{1}{4} = \dfrac{3}{4}$

$\dfrac{1}{2} + \dfrac{2}{8} = \dfrac{3}{4}$

$\dfrac{7}{9} - \dfrac{4}{6} = \dfrac{1}{9}$

$\dfrac{2}{4} + \dfrac{2}{4} = \dfrac{4}{4}$

$\dfrac{1}{2} - \dfrac{2}{8} = \dfrac{1}{4}$

$\dfrac{1}{2} + \dfrac{1}{2} = 1$

PART IV

Mathematical Pathways Through Literature

Grade One / Treasure Sorts

Grade Two / Money Matters

Grade Three / One for You, One for Me

Grade Four / Strategies

Grade Five / More or Less

Grade Six / Looking at Decimals

Treasure Sorts

Exploring Common Attributes

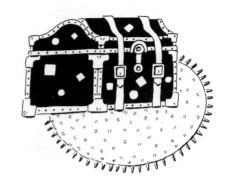

MATERIALS

Kit:

■ 50-75 buttons of different sizes, colors, textures, numbers of holes

Supplies:

■ full sheets of paper

PREPARATION

Cut tagboard or paper into 1" × 3" cards.

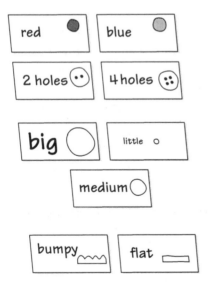

1 Have students sit in a circle. Put a collection of buttons in the center. Ask, *What are some things you notice about the buttons?* Let the children suggest several attributes. *All the things you noticed are* attributes *of the buttons. I'll write some of the attributes on these cards.* On 1" × 3" cards, record a variety of attributes, such as color, size, shape, and number of holes.

2 Introduce the game. Have everyone take a button. Draw one large ring on a full sheet of paper. Select one attribute card, and place it inside the ring. If the card reads, "blue," for example, say, *When we put this card here, it means all buttons that are blue go in the ring. All buttons that are not blue go outside the ring.* Go around the circle asking, *Where does your button belong?* and having children place their buttons inside or outside the ring. Repeat the activity with different cards until the children seem confident sorting by one attribute.

3 Introduce the two-ring game. Mix up the buttons, and have each child take one. On a full sheet of paper draw two large overlapping rings. Choose two attribute cards, and place one card in each ring, asking, *What does this card mean?* Repeat the Treasure Sorts game, asking each child, *Where does your button belong?*

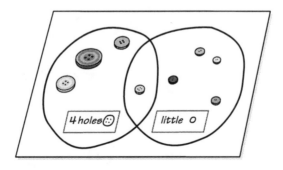

LITERATURE PATH

The Button Box is a unique sorting and classifying book—a treasure to share with students. Pages of buttons, grouped by a variety of attributes, will encourage students to consider different ways to organize collections and sets. Many other picture books encourage attribute sorting. Look for ways for children to sort and count clothing, animals, trees, or other illustrations. Sorting encourages vocabulary development as children discover new ways of describing groups.

The Button Box

by Margarette S. Reid and illustrated by Sarah Chamberlain

The Button Box is a fascinating look at an object so familiar to everyone that it is seldom thought about at all. Each group of buttons has a story to tell. Grandma's special collection is a box of memories that has been put together over many years.

The illustrations invite the reader to scoop up a handful of buttons and take a closer look.

Ms. Reid's suggestions for child-pleasing ways to use buttons are too much fun to pass up. Making button spinners, like the one in the book, is almost a lost art today. It's a simple, old-fashioned toy that will delight children and bring back memories for adults. Sock puppets with shank button eyes are great boring-day companions. After reading the final page, *Buttons, Buttons, Who Invented Buttons?* an interesting history lesson, the buttons in your life will take on new meaning.

ENJOYING THE READING EXPERIENCE

Have you thought about the buttons in your life? Not everyone has. To introduce this book, ask students to examine the buttons on their shirts and blouses and compare them with all the other buttons they see. After the story, review some of the descriptive button words in the book and use them in different sorting activities so they can be added to every student's verbal toolbox. Talk about other collection boxes that would be fun to start.

BUTTON UP!

Every child loves a treasure box, and in Margarette S. Reid's *Button Box*, there are buttons for every occasion. They're flowered and carved, made from shell and sand. After students look at the first picture and guess what's inside the box, they will need time to study the pages and comment on the different sorting arrangements they see.

After reading the book, it's time to bring out your own collection of buttons. Each child chooses a button from the box. After imagining what kind of clothing the button would come from, the student draws a picture of the clothing. For a final touch, the button should be drawn so it looks like it's sewn in place on a garment. If time allows, encourage the children to write or dictate a story about their buttons.

MYSTERY BUTTONS

So that students have more opportunities to take part in this guessing game, divide them into groups of ten or fewer. When a group is seated in a circle, place a pile of buttons in the center of the group. The buttons are spread out so all of them can be seen. The person who is "it" mentally selects a button without touching it, or telling anyone which one was chosen. Attributes are given as hints, one at a time, until someone in the circle guesses the mystery button.

The teacher should be the first button selector so students have a model to follow. Some students may need to discuss the different attributes the buttons have before they begin the game.

Example:

My button has two holes.
My button is shiny.
My button is square.
My button is red.

Money Madness

Solving Money Problems

PREPARATION

Make a chart like the one pictured below.

Beach Street Boardwalk
10 Tickets for $1.00

Ferris Wheel	5 Tickets
Bumper Cars	3 Tickets
Roller Coasters	3 Tickets
Ring Toss	2 Tickets
Ring the Bell	2 Tickets

1 Tell students, *Today, we're off for a day at an imaginary beach boardwalk. We've got $2 to spend. Let's plan our day.* Show the class the chart you made. Talk about the events on the list.

- *How many tickets do you need to ride the Ferris wheel?*
- *What things can you do for 2 tickets?*
- *How many tickets can you buy for a dollar?*

2 *Pretend that everyone has $2 to spend on tickets. I want each of you to make a plan that tells which tickets you would buy and what you would do at the boardwalk. Write a report to tell about your plan.*

3 At the end of math time, let the children share their plans for a day at the Beach Street Boardwalk.

Bumper Cars 3 20
Bumper Cars 3
Bumper Cars 3
Bumper Cars 3
Bumper Cars 3
Bumper Cars 3
Ring the Bell 2

Ferris Wheel 5 tickets
3 tickets
3 tickets
3 tickets
3 tickets
Bumper cars 3 tickets

today I Had
21 tickets
R 3 ticket
R 3 ticket
R 3 tike+
R 3 ticket
R 3 ticket
R 3 tick
R 3 ticket

LITERATURE PATH

Characters in stories have problems to solve. Arthur, in *Arthur's Funny Money*, needs money. He plans, with his sister's ideas, a way to earn it and he almost accomplishes his goal. *The Three Billy Goats Gruff* are looking for greener pastures, and *Peter Rabbit* finds himself trapped in Mr. MacGregor's garden, a candidate for rabbit pie. Reread favorite stories for a second look at the problems characters face. Discuss the solutions given in the books. Ask students to put themselves in the character's place and see if they can suggest more effective ways to deal with the same problems.

Arthur's Funny Money

by Lillian Hoban

Arthur is determined to earn enough money to buy a Far Out Frisbees T-shirt and matching cap. Little sister Violet supplies the young entrepreneur with ideas and helps keep track of the money. Violet records their transactions, but Arthur can't determine the balance in his piggy bank account. Will there be enough money for the shirt and cap? Will Violet find the answer to her own number problem? Tune in to *Arthur's Funny Money* for an entertaining financial lesson with a licorice twist.

ENJOYING THE READING EXPERIENCE

Introduce Arthur to the class before reading the story. Explain that he wants to buy a Far Out Frisbees T-shirt and matching cap. He doesn't have enough money. Ask students to suggest ways he could earn the money.

After reading the story, give Violet equal time. Use pencils or crayons to represent the licorice sticks and have students act out Violet's math problem. Discuss the outcome of the licorice exchange. Arthur's calculations are correct, yet he still finds himself with one piece of licorice and Violet with four. Talk about the equal shares of licorice on the last page of the story.

IT MAKES CENTS

Read *Arthur's Funny Money* through page 54. On a posted sheet of chart paper write, ***Can You Help Arthur With His Money Problems?*** and the following problems for the children to solve.

1. *If Arthur has $3.78 and needs $5.00 to buy a Far Out Frisbees T-shirt and matching hat, how much money does he need to earn?*
2. *Arthur had $3.78, but he spent 53¢ for soap and 27¢ for a box of Brillo pads. How much money does he have now? How much more money does he need to buy his T-shirt and hat?*
3. *Bubbles ate some of the soap and Brillo pads. Norman gave Arthur 42¢ for washing his bike and trike. Was this a fair deal? Explain why or why not.*
4. *Arthur washed bikes and toys. Wilma gave Arthur 34¢; Peter gave Arthur 36¢; and John gave Arthur 33¢. How much money does Arthur have now?*

Give children several days to find the answers to the questions on the chart. They could pair-up, or work in teams of four, to find the solutions. After everyone has had a chance to put Arthur's financial records in order, finish reading the story. Children can compare their answers with the information in the book.

GOODS AND SERVICES

Have students think of ways they could spend $5.00 and ways to earn that amount of money. Remind them that some projects will cost money for supplies. After students decide what they want to do, let them estimate or find the cost of needed supplies. Then challenge them to determine how much they will charge for their services or products. When the price is set, have the students find out how many times they'll have to perform the service, or how many items they must sell, to earn $5.00. Don't expect the children's figuring to be exact. Praise their thinking and their efforts.

One for You, One for Me

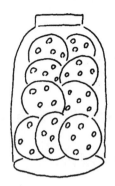

Writing Division Equations

MATERIALS

Supplies:

■ full sheets of drawing paper

1 *Imagine you had a dozen cookies to share with three of your friends. How many cookies would each of you get? Talk over the problem with a partner. Draw a picture showing how you solved it.* When students have finished, let them tell how they solved the problem.

2 *We can write the equation 12 ÷ 4 = 3 to describe this problem.* Write it on the chalkboard. *What do you think this equation means?* Let several students give their ideas. Encourage them to relate the numbers in the problem to the way they solved the problem. Finally, present several variations of the cookie problem for students to try. With each new problem, challenge the students to draw pictures and write an equation.

- *How would you and your partner share 12 cookies fairly with 5 friends?*
- *What about 2 friends?*
- *What about 4 friends?*

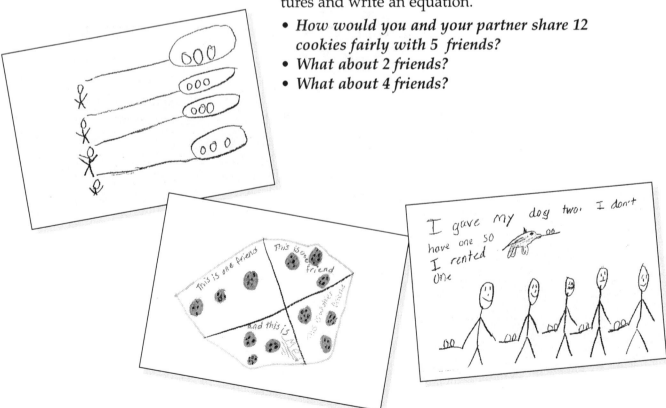

LITERATURE PATH

The first time *The Doorbell Rang* in Victoria and Sam's house there were plenty of cookies to share with guests. But each time someone new came, the shares got smaller. This humorous story keeps readers dividing and calculating throughout the book. It points out the importance of equal shares. Challenge students to keep on the lookout for other ways characters in books share things equally.

The Doorbell Rang

by Pat Hutchins

Who's at the door? Pat Hutchins keeps everyone guessing in her cookie-sharing book, *The Doorbell Rang*. One plate of six cookies for each is the right number until two friends ring the bell. Now there are four plates with three cookies each. Before anyone can manage a bite, more friends file in the door. The share grows smaller and smaller until Grandma saves the day, and we all know that no one makes cookies like Grandma.

ENJOYING THE READING EXPERIENCE

Introduce the book by passing out food samples to the class. Give one student two extra pieces and see what happens. When the complaints are heard, ask what can be done so everyone has a fair share. After the discussion, distribute two extra pieces to the rest of the class. During the second reading, students follow the passing of time in the pictures. What is the cat doing during the story? What items are left by the door? Even the teapot and coffee pot are part of the action.

ON STAGE

Sharing is the theme of Pat Hutchins' delightful book, *The Doorbell Rang*. Invite the students to act out the story. After practicing, it's time to take the show on the road! The children perform *The Doorbell Rang* for another class. If there are cookies for the children in both classes, everyone will have a good time. Before they go, the students need to find out how many dozen cookies they should take. Let students do the cookie calculations!

GRANDMA'S COOKIES

Cookie-solving problems are a high interest activity for third grade students. In *The Doorbell Rang*, there are 12 children at the kitchen table when the story ends. How many cookies would Grandma have to bring so everyone has two cookies? Three? Four?

If Grandma's recipe makes six dozen, how many cookies would each child have? If the class divided six dozen cookies equally, how many cookies could each student eat? Are there any extras for the teacher?

Invite students to write their own cookie problems for their classmates to solve. Encourage them to use multiplication or division equations to find the answers.

Strategies

Building a Network of
Number Relationships

MATERIALS

Supplies:

■ full sheets and half-sheets of
paper; calculator

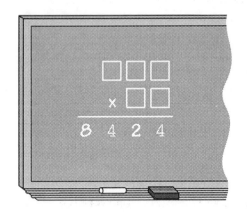

1 On the chalkboard, draw a "blank" multiplication problem with the answer 8424 written in, as shown at left. Say, *Here's a problem for you to solve. Can you arrange the digits 1, 2, 3, 4, and 5 in these boxes so that when the numbers are multiplied the answer is 8424?* Make sure the students understand that each digit may be used only once. *Work with your partner and use your calculator to solve the problem.*

2 Allow students time to solve the problem. Then talk about some of the strategies the pairs used.

- *How many tries did it take you to figure out the answer?*
- *How did you keep track of your guesses?*
- *What strategies did you use to help you solve the problem?*

3 *Now it's your turn to create some challenging multiplication problems for your classmates to solve.* Each pair should make up a problem (for example, 351 × 24) and figure out the answer. They should then draw a multiplication equation with boxes for digits and with the product written in. Finally, they should make a list of the digits needed to complete the equation.

4 Collect the problems students created and put them into a hat or bag. Let each pair draw out one problem to solve. *When you have solved the problem double-check your answer with the calculator. Make sure your answer is reasonable. Then you may draw a new problem to work on.*

5 At the end of math time, have the students choose one of the problems they solved, and write about the strategies.

LITERATURE PATH

As students work with *Math-a-Magic,* they learn to pull information from the printed page and turn it into action. This will improve the reading techniques needed in all subject areas. How-to craft and art books and a supply of materials for some of the projects in the books will strengthen students' reading-to-find-out skills. Books that explain how to perform magic tricks are another kid-friendly way to work on reading skills.

Math-a-Magic

by Laurence B. White, Jr. and Ray Broekel; illustrated by Meyer Seltzer

Fun is the only way to describe the magical number games in *Math-a-Magic.* It's all there for young magicians, including the jokes to entertain the audience. Spectators will say, *wow,* followed by *how?* Of course, real magicians never tell. Those who want to be in on the secret will have to read the book for themselves. *Math-a-Magic* is filled with page after page of useful information, including how to find out the teacher's age.

ENJOYING THE READING EXPERIENCE

To introduce the book, point out the three sections under each magical math trick. There is "The Trick," "How to Do It," and "The *Math-a-Magic* Secret." Select one of the magic tricks and read the sections one at a time. After each section, ask the students to sum-up the directions so they will have a better understanding of how to follow the instructions.

HOCUS POCUS

The numerical magic tricks in *Math-a-Magic* will keep students figuring all year. To get them off to a good start, list all the titles of the tricks on a large sheet of paper. Students will pair up for this activity. Have the pairs choose one of the titles from the list without looking at the book. On a rotating basis, have students read only about the magic trick they selected. They should record what they need to do to perform their numerical magic trick. Remind them to note any funny stories or information for the audience.

Allow practice time after the students have written the directions for performing their *Math-a-Magic* tricks. Read the "Patter's Important" section on page 5 to the class. Ask each team to work on a patter to go with their act. When everyone is ready, set a date for the performance. Invite another class, school workers, or parents to come to the *Math-a-Magic* show.

EASY AS ONE, TWO, THREE

Ask pairs of students to select another *Math-a-Magic* trick. The directions in the book are written in narrative form. The teams should read the directions and rewrite the essential steps in a numbered, easy-to-follow form. Ask students to write the directions in as few steps as possible while still enabling the trick to be performed.

When all the teams have completed their directions, put the directions in a hat (or a box). Invite each team to draw a *Math-a-Magic* trick from the hat. If they draw their own, have them exchange or draw another. After a practice session, the teams perform their magic trick by following the directions on the papers. If some pairs experience difficulty following the directions, encourage them to ask the authors of the directions for clarity. After the performance, discuss what happened when they tried to follow the simplified directions.

More or Less?

Developing Probability Sense

....

MATERIALS

Kit:

■ a deck of playing cards for each group of four

Supplies:

■ full sheets of paper

PREPARATION

Copy the rules for playing "More or Less?", shown below, onto chart paper.

....

How to Play "More or Less?"

• Partners need a deck of cards. Each player is dealt 5 cards from the shuffled deck. Players decide who will play for sums more than 10 and who for sums less than or equal to 10.

• Each player turns one card face up. If the sum of the numbers is 10 or less, that player gets a point. If the sum of the numbers is more than 10, that player gets a point.

• Players continue until all the cards have been played. The winner is the player with the most points.

---

11 and up won because there is only 20 numbers for 10 and down, but there is much more of a chance for 11 and up (5) if we were to play 500 more times I think the results would still be 11 and up wins!

1 *Today we're going to play a card game in which two players each turn over a card. One player scores a point for sums that are more than 10, and the other player scores a point for sums equal to or less than 10. Which player do you think will win most often?* Have students explain their thinking.

2 *Let's see how your predictions hold up.* Refer students to the rules you posted on chart paper. Have a volunteer help demonstrate the game.

3 Have students play 10 rounds of this game with a partner and record the results of each round, including whether they were playing for more than 10 or for 10 or less. After students have finished playing the game, have them write about what happened, including mathematical statements about the probability of each player's winning and how that affects the fairness of the game.

4 At the end of math time, discuss the students' experiences and their conclusions.

• *Did you most often get a sum of more than 10 or of 10 or less? Will this always happen? Why or why not?*

• *What did you find when you figured out all of the possible outcomes?*

• *Can you figure out a way to win this game all the time? Most of the time? How did you do it?*

• *Can you figure out a way to make this game more fair for both players?*

Soothsayers, palm readers, and stargazers have made predictions about the future for thousands of years. People have searched the sky for signs that would predict the weather. There are omens that predict good and bad fortune. Ask students to share stories they find in the library, both fact and fiction, that involve predictions. They'll find several examples in Greek myths and the familiar *Sleeping Beauty*.

Do You Wanna Bet?
Your Chance to Find Out about Probability

by Jean Cushman and illustrated by Martha Weston

Talk about luck! Danny and Brian, two good friends, do. They discuss their chances all through the book and discover what the odds are. Will Danny have a baby brother or sister? You have to read through the book to find out. How do weather forecasters predict rain or shine? How do you break the code? What can you do to win at cards and Monopoly? Which games should you play at the carnival? These are secrets everyone should know.

ENJOYING THE READING EXPERIENCE

Bring a basketful of good luck charms to class. Discuss the odds of good luck or bad luck on Friday the Thirteenth. Have students comment on good and bad fortune and their chances for each. Examine the items in the basket and let the students decide if anything they see would help them improve their grades in school. To introduce the book, read about probability and the toss of the coin on pages 1-6. Students will enjoy returning to the book from time to time to check on their chances. When baseball season is in the air, they can refer to "Baseball Statistics and Strategy."

YOU CAN TALK ABOUT IT

Read pages 13-15 in *Do You Wanna Bet? Your Chance to Find Out about Probability* to the class. After reading the selection, review the information on page 14 that explains how forecasters make predictions: observing what is happening outside, finding out what is happening at the source of the weather system, and comparing what happened when there were similar conditions in the past. Have students explain how the weather percentages are calculated from this information. Discuss the predictability of certain weather conditions in the community during the year.

Have students listen to the weather predictions on radio or TV for a week. They should record the prediction including the percentages. Then, below the prediction, they should record the actual weather conditions that occurred on that day. Discuss the accuracy of the predictions and the percentages that were given by the forecasters.

THE ODDS-ON FAVORITE

What are the odds? It's time to find out. Pair up the students and have them select a probability experiment from, *Do You Wanna Bet?* Have pairs write out the directions in a numbered, step-by-step format. Allow students a half-hour with the book. Some groups may need a few minutes longer, however. On a central list, ask students to record the name of the activity they chose. After they test their directions and try the experiment, have them share the results with the rest of the class.

Looking at Decimals

Exploring Decimals

MATERIALS

Supplies:

■ scratch paper; calculator

PREPARATION

Construct a large paper number line. (Ten continuous sheets of computer paper hung horizontally will work well.) Label the number line 1 at the beginning and 10 at the end, with the rest of the numbers 2-9 at regular intervals in between. Post the number line where the class can see it.

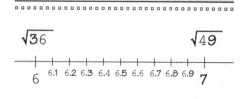

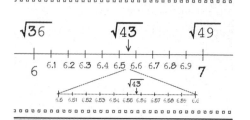

1 Point out the number line you posted. On the board write $\sqrt{25}$. *Here's a number that goes somewhere on our number line. We say, "the square root of 25." It represents some number that, multiplied by itself, is equal to 25. What number times itself is 25? Since $\sqrt{25}$ is another name for 5, let's put that number on our number line above the number 5.*

2 Present other squares of whole numbers, and for each number have the students tell you what the square root is and where it belongs on the number line. (Some students may need to use their calculators.)

3 On the board, write $\sqrt{43}$. *Here's a number that goes somewhere on our number line. Let's try to figure out where. What number times itself is 43?* After students work for awhile with their calculators, ask where to place $\sqrt{43}$ on the number line. Someone is likely to suggest that the answer is between 6 and 7.

4 *You don't have fraction keys on your calculator, so you can't try multiplying 6 1/2 by itself. But you can multiply with decimal numbers on your calculator.* List on the number line, between 6 and 7, the decimal numbers 6.1 through 6.9 *Which of these numbers is halfway between 6 and 7? Enter that number with its decimal point on your calculator. Multiply that number by itself and see what you get. Keep going with new decimal numbers until you come close to a number which is the square root of 43.* Have students continue working until they have narrowed the field of possibilities for $\sqrt{43}$ to between 6.55 and 6.56. Draw a line in the space between 6.55 and 6.56 to indicate placement and label the arrow $\sqrt{43}$.

The Phantom Tollbooth is one fiction book with a lot of mathematical discoveries to be investigated. Take a return journey to Digitopolis and rediscover all the mathematical nonsense and magic that takes place there. Challenge the students to look for and create mathematical discoveries for characters in other literature books.

The Phantom Tollbooth

by Norton Juster and illustrated by Jules Feiffer

Milo, a boy who hasn't developed a zest for learning or anything else, finds a mysterious package in his room when he comes home from school. He follows the directions for putting the contents together, *One Genuine Turnpike Tollbooth,* and sets out in his small, electric automobile for Dictionopolis, located near the foothills of Confusion and the Doldrums. After several wild adventures with his friends, Tock the ticking dog and Humbug, Milo manages to bring Rhyme and Reason back to the Kingdom of Wisdom. When he returns home, he discovers a world of exciting things to do, right where he left them.

ENJOYING THE READING EXPERIENCE

As an introduction to the story, read page 9 and part of page 11. Stop reading when Milo says, *"Another long afternoon."* Ask students to describe their impressions of Milo and to tell why they think he felt the way he did.

Students may be unfamiliar with the meaning of many words in the book. Take time to talk about the vocabulary at the beginning of each chapter so they don't miss out on the fun.

AN AVERAGE FAMILY

Review Chapter 16, "A Very Dirty Bird" in *The Phantom Tollbooth*. The boy Milo talks to is just 58% there. It isn't strange, the boy explains, because every family has 2.58 children. He just happens to be the ".58" in his family. Discuss these averages with the class. To review averages, write the following sentence on the overhead projector: *Every 100 families would have 258 children*. Display a grid with 100 squares to represent the families. Write a number in each square to represent the children in that family. The numbers in the squares must add up to 258.

Develop a set of five survey questions with the class. Some possiblities might be:

- *How many children are in your family? (Remember to include yourself.)*
- *How many pets does your family have?*
- *How many cars (or TV sets) does your family have?*
- *Do you live in a house, a condominium, an apartment, or a townhouse?*

Print up the survey with a space for each of the answers. Emphasize that the survey results are confidential—no names need to be included. Ask teachers of fourth or fifth-graders to distribute the surveys to their classes. When the surveys are returned, have your students help you tally the results on a chart, and work out the averages. Compare the average number of children in each family in the survey to the average in *The Phantom Tollbooth*.

MORE OR LESS

After silently choosing a decimal number, begin a guessing game by saying, *"I'm thinking of a decimal number between one and twenty. Can you guess my number?"* Allow students to ask ten questions to try to find the number. For example, someone might ask, *"Is it 7.5?"* You must be able to answer the questions with *"It's greater than...or it's less than...."* If someone guesses the number, that person takes your place, and the game begins again.

The range of possible numbers can be adjusted, but it will be easier to begin with numbers between one and twenty. Once students understand the game, divide them into playing groups of six so each student will have more opportunities to play.

Writing Math

Our Favorites

MATHEMATICS FOCUS

Representing Data

Organizing information makes it easier to discuss and interpret. Data can be presented using pictures and symbols.

Children make up three questions about favorites to ask the class. They draw pictures to answer the questions, sort the data, and present it on a poster.

....

MATERIALS

❏ chart paper

❏ eighth sheets of paper

❏ three legal-size envelopes

❏ 12" x 18" drawing paper

❏ scissors

❏ paste

PREPARATION Tape each legal-size envelope to an $8\frac{1}{2}$" x 11" sheet of paper. Before the second session, copy sets of the class's data.

TIME 4 sessions

WRITING FOCUS

Interpreting Favorites

Putting thoughts into drawing and writing and noting how a sentence begins and ends are two of the first steps to becoming writers.

Children interpret information on their posters, then write complete sentences to report their findings.

....

MATERIALS

❏ chart paper

❏ writing paper

TIME 1 session

Representing Data

Finding ways to organize our answers and report them is the big challenge.

ASKING QUESTIONS

1 *Let's see what we can find out about each other's favorite things.* Take a quick poll to find out the children's favorite colors. Write the results on the chalkboard. *What other "favorites" questions could we ask to learn more about each other?* Write on chart paper the children's suggestions, and read them aloud.

2 Choose three questions for the class to answer. Write each of the three questions on an envelope. Post the envelopes where everyone can reach them. *For each question, draw an answer and put your name on it. Put each drawing in the envelope for the question it answers.*

3 At the end of math time, tell the class that, starting tomorrow, they will look at everyone's answers and see what they can find out.

4 Before the next math time, arrange each envelope's answers on an 11″ × 17″ sheet of paper and photocopy the three sets for each pair.

LOOKING AT ANSWERS

5 Each day, meet at the rug. Spread out the answers from one envelope and talk about what the children notice.

- *Do you see the drawing you made?*

- *Do you see some that are like yours? that are different?*

- *What is a way we could sort these answers?* Sort the pictures according to several suggestions.

- *How many favorites are something sweet, like a dessert?* Ask other *How many?* questions.

6 At their seats, have pairs cut apart the photocopied answers for the day's questions, organize them on drawing paper, and paste them down. Help each pair write on their poster a sentence that begins: "We found out _____." Post the children's recordings on the wall.

Interpreting Favorites

Our walls are covered with posters! Now we write about what we learn from them.

GATHERING DATA FROM POSTERS

1 Focus the children's attention on the posters in general. Then spend some time talking about individual posters.

- *Who can tell us something about the favorites of our class by looking at these posters?*

- *How many different favorite things have we shown on our posters?*

- *On this poster, which (animal) did most of you choose?*

- *What are the different categories on this poster?*

REPORTING ON OUR OWN

Favorites

Lots of kids like pizza best.

Only one person likes turtles best of all.

Six different animals were said.

2 *Let's make a report about our favorites. What are some things we know about our favorites?* Write the children's responses on chart paper. Use the children's exact language, encouraging them to put their ideas into complete sentences.

3 As you write the children's sentences, informally talk about appropriate capitalization, punctuation, and spacing of words.

- *What does this mark at the end of the sentence mean?*

- *Why did I make this a big "L"?*

- *Why is there a space here and here in this sentence?*

4 *Now it's your turn to be writers.* Have the children write about something they learned about the class favorites.

> You will observe a wide variation in children's writing skills–drawings, strings of letters, individual words, complete thoughts, and a mixture of invented and conventional spelling. Some children may just copy the sentences written on the chart paper. Show your appreciation and enjoyment of all the children's writing.

BEGINNING THE REVISION PROCESS

5 When the children finish writing, focus their attention on their own papers. *Point to where you wrote your name on your writing.* Make sure all the children include their names.

> The simple step of checking that their names are on their papers helps children become acquainted with the revision stage of the writing process and promotes a sense of authorship.

SHARING OUR REPORTS

6 Provide time for the students to share their writing with the class. You may want to do this in short sessions throughout the day or over the next few days.

> It is important that the children's writing be honored–given a moment in the spotlight before the class, on a library shelf, or at home with family members. Make time in this first writing activity for all the children to share their writing with the class. As they share, you will also have the opportunity to model listening and responding skills.

ASSESSMENT

This first writing endeavor will let you evaluate where each child is in his understanding of the written language.

- *Did the child use words or pictures to communicate meaning?*
- *Did the child report his thinking?*

(Classroom Talk)

MODELING

Modeling is an effective teaching strategy. Writing and thinking aloud in front of the children allows them to construct for themselves the meaning and importance of writing. In addition, modeling allows the teacher the opportunity to experience the kind of thinking involved in the writing experience.

In this lesson, model making statements about the class's favorites expressed in complete sentences. As you write the children's own words on chart paper, model appropriate writing mechanics. Be sure to think aloud as you are writing.

- *I'll begin this sentence with a capital letter.*
- *'Turtle', that starts with 't'.*

How to Cut a Cake

MATHEMATICS FOCUS

Making Fair Shares

A single object shared equally can be used to model fractions. It is possible to make fair shares of a whole. There may be many ways to divide one whole into the same number of equal parts.

Children draw pictures to show cakes cut into fair shares for different numbers of people. The results are discussed, and the pages of cake drawings bound into books.

....

MATERIALS

❑ chart paper

❑ full sheets of paper

❑ colored markers or crayons

❑ supplies for covering and binding books

PREPARATION Copy onto chart paper the list of possible cakes (see page 31). You may wish to bring in a sheet cake for sharing.

TIME 1-2 sessions

WRITING FOCUS

Giving Directions

Directions for cutting a cake should include a list of things needed, steps for how to do it, and helpful illustrations.

Children discuss what they know about directions and their ideas for writing directions. Pairs write directions for cutting a cake fairly, try to follow another pair's directions, and talk about the results.

....

MATERIALS

❑ writing paper

❑ scissors

PREPARATION Cut out paper "cake tops" (some round and some rectangular), enough for each pair to have two identical shapes. Bring in commercial directions for recipes, games, and crafts to discuss.

TIME 2 sessions

Making Fair Shares

We're going to be experts on cutting cakes.

SLICING THE SERVINGS

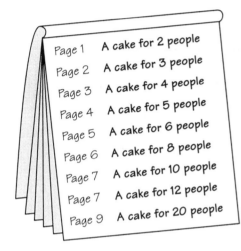

Page 1   A cake for 2 people
Page 2   A cake for 3 people
Page 3   A cake for 4 people
Page 4   A cake for 5 people
Page 5   A cake for 6 people
Page 6   A cake for 8 people
Page 7   A cake for 10 people
Page 7   A cake for 12 people
Page 9   A cake for 20 people

1   *Today we're going to make our own books called, "How to Cut a Cake." Each page will tell something different.* Show the class the chart paper and let children pick the different pages they want to do.

2   *Draw a cake and pick the number of servings you'll make. Show how to divide your cake so everyone gets a fair share. Write how many people your cake is for.* Let children do as many pages as they like.

3   At the end of math time, talk about what the children did.

- *What can you say about cake cutting?*
- *What was the easiest cake to cut? the hardest? Why?*
- *Did you cut your cake differently from someone else who cut a cake into the same number of servings?*

MAKING BOOKS

4   Bind the papers together into individual books titled, *How to Cut a Cake.*

You may want to end this week of sharing by bringing in a sheet cake for the children to enjoy. If so, prepare papers the size of the actual cake and challenge the children to figure out a way to cut the cake so that everyone in the class gets a fair share.

Giving Directions

We'll find out whether writing directions is as easy as we think it is.

THINKING IT THROUGH

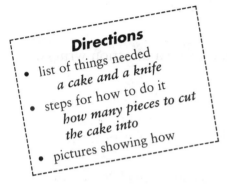

Directions
- list of things needed
  a cake and a knife
- steps for how to do it
  how many pieces to cut
  the cake into
- pictures showing how

WRITING DIRECTIONS

1 Talk with the children about what they know about directions. *Have you ever used directions to help you play a new game or make something? What are some things your directions included?* Take children's responses, then show the class the commercial directions you have provided and discuss what they include.

2 *Talk with your partner about the types of things you would need to include if you were going to write directions for sharing a cake.* Ask pairs to share with the class some of their ideas. Record suggestions on chart paper.

3 Provide each pair of children with two matching cake cut-outs. Explain that one cake cut-out is for them to cut as they are deciding how and thinking about the steps. Later, they'll give the other cake cut-out to another pair who will cut it as they follow the directions they are given.

4 *Work with your partner to decide how many pieces to cut your cake into and how your cake should be cut fairly. Then write directions that will help someone else cut the cake exactly as you have.*

5 Remind the children that their directions should tell what is to be done and include a list of things needed, steps for how to do it, and pictures showing how to do it.

REVISING DIRECTIONS

6 When the pairs are finished writing their directions, have the partners reread their directions aloud to each other.

- *Are your directions clear?*
- *Are your illustrations helpful?*
- *Do you think another pair will be able to read your directions and cut the cake exactly as you have?*

STEP BY STEP

7 Have the pairs exchange directions and the uncut cakes. *Follow the directions exactly as you cut the cake.*

8 When the children are finished cutting cakes, have them return the cake pieces to the original direction writers. Talk about the results.

- *Was the cake cut as you expected? If not, why not?*
- *How could your directions have been more clear?*
- *Did any pair not follow the directions exactly? Explain what happened.*
- *Was it easier to write directions or follow directions?*

ASSESSMENT

To assess this writing activity, evaluate how well the pairs communicate their understanding of fair shares in clearly written directions.

- *Were the pair's directions clear and the illustrations helpful?*
- *Did the directions describe a cake cut into fair shares?*

(Classroom Talk)

USING DISCOURSE TO PROMOTE THINKING

Children's thinking is revealed as they verbalize ideas. Exchanging ideas, the children engage in processes of metacognition—monitoring, regulating, and evaluating. Participation in groups and in whole class discussions helps children generate new ideas and transfer what is learned to new situations with greater success.

In this lesson, partners discuss the elements of well written directions, then the children share their thinking in a class discussion. The record made of the class's ideas is a richer one than would be lists generated by the children individually.

Animal Research

MATHEMATICS FOCUS

Displaying Data

Mathematics is used in many ways in the world around us. Problem solving can be especially meaningful when applied to real-world settings.

Students research animals, collecting numerical data. This information is displayed in a large class database, then students estimate figures to fill in any empty cells.

••••••••••••••••••••••••••••••••••••

MATERIALS

❑ Animals of the Zoo cards

❑ push pins

❑ inch rulers and foot measuring tapes

PREPARATION Gather resource books.

TIME 3 sessions

WRITING FOCUS

Reporting On Animals

Formats for note taking and structuring paragraphs are effective ways to collect and organize information about animals for a report.

Students brainstorm topics to research, then learn a format for organizing their notes. They write and edit reports which are shared and displayed.

••••••••••••••••••••••••••••••••••••

MATERIALS

❑ writing paper

❑ supplies for report covers

PREPARATION Resource books should be available. Make a copy for each student of Editing Checklist (page 188).

TIME 4 sessions

Animal Data Table

Animal	Weight at Birth	Adult Weight	Height	Length	Number of Babies	Grou Size
lion	3 or 4 lbs				1 to 6	
heron	72 kg		4 ft.			8—5
brown bear			9 ft.			8 to 5
polar bear				5-12 ft		
vulture	12 to 13 lbs				1	7
red deer		30 to 50 lbs				
iguana				12 inches		
toucan						

Use yarn lengths to set up the grid for your Animal Data Table. Cut full sheets of paper into quarters widthwise for the strips. Put the column headings up. Row headings will be added by the students.

Displaying Data

Our research is focused on numbers, as we gather data to compare animals to each other.

PLANNING THE DISPLAYS

TRACKING DOWN THE FACTS

Can we use information that we have to make educated guesses about the missing information?

I bet a lion is about the same as a tiger. We know how tall a tiger is —about 3 feet.

Right. So a lion is about 3 feet tall, too.

What does everyone else think?

1 *We're going to pretend to be animal researchers this week.* Have each pair draw a card from the bag of Animal of the Zoo cards and think of several clues they could use to describe the animal. Go around the class letting each pair give two or three clues about their animal.

2 Point out the grid on the bulletin board. *Our challenge is to complete this table of animal information. Your job is to research your Zoo card animal and fill in as many cells as you can with data for your animal.* Have each pair write the name of their animal on a strip and pin it in the first column of the chart to form row headings.

3 Next, point out the column headings on the table. *As you read about your animals, keep your eyes open for this information. Add it to our data table as you find it.* (Have strips and push pins available near the table.)

4 For the next few days, students will need to share the Animals of the Zoo cards and the resource books. Try to keep the class focused on inches and feet, instead of metric measurements.

5 At the end of math time each day, bring the class together to share ideas.

- *What's the most interesting thing you've learned so far?*
- *How did you know where to place information in the table?*

6 When students have added all of their data to the table, suggest they use logical thinking to make educated guesses about the missing information, then fill in the empty cells.

Reporting On Animals

Now we organize our animal data into report form and learn different aspects of the editing process.

GATHERING INFORMATION

How do they eat without teeth?	who are their enemies?
What do they need to live in zoos?	How do they take care of their babies?

WRITING THE REPORT

Report Format

- **Paragraph One:** general information about the animal

- **Paragraphs Two-Five:** specific information about one of the questions

- **Paragraph Six:** general summary information

1 Explain to the students that they will each write a report about their favorite animal. *Take five minutes and write all you know about your animal.* Have students share what they have written with a partner.

2 *Now take a few minutes to write down things you would like to learn about your animal.* For this report, have students choose four questions to research.

3 Demonstrate how to fold a paper into fourths and head each section for note taking. *As you find information that answers your questions, jot a few words in the appropriate box to help you remember it.*

While students are engaged in research, encourage them to use the library and librarian's help to search for specific information. You may want to have a mini-lesson on using the index and table of contents to help locate specific information in a book.

4 *Once you have found the information that answers your questions, organize each question and the information into a paragraph with three or four sentences.* Explain that the first paragraph of the report should provide general information about the animal, while the following three or four paragraphs should relate information pertaining to the questions the student had.

Students will require varying amounts of time to gather information and write their reports. Expect that some children will finish in one or two days, while others will take several days.

EDITING TO DISPLAY 5 Schedule three mini-lessons to focus on aspects of the editing process. Have students use the appropriate section of the Editing Checklist for each.

FOR YOUR INFORMATION 6 Invite students to make decorative covers for their reports. Display the reports on a bulletin board or in the classroom or school library. Include in the reports a page at the end for comments from readers.

ASSESSMENT To assess this writing activity, evaluate how well students communicate their interpretation of data in a report.

- *Did the student effectively formulate questions and locate information?*
- *Is the report well organized?*

(Classroom Talk)

TALKING ABOUT REPORTS

As students work through the steps of report writing, provide ample time for them to talk about what they are learning. These opportunities for productive talk have two goals: that students internalize the information they gather, and that they trust they have something to say. Having this foundation will help students write their reports using their own voice, rather than copying from sources. Here are some recommended activities.

- Begin sessions with five minutes of free writing in which students write without notes "to get to know what they know."
- Alternately, begin sessions by having students write for five minutes, using their notes to formulate complete sentences.
- Start or end sessions with peer interviews, in which students ask each other questions about their topics and use what they remember and their notes to respond.
- End sessions with a class discussion about problems students are encountering. Have students offer suggestions or share information to help others solve their problems.
- Have peers conference about revising and editing.

EDITING CHECKLIST

SESSION ONE

Checking for Organization and Readability

• Read your report aloud to yourself.

_____ Does your report have four or five paragraphs?

_____ Does each paragraph have a topic sentence and at least three supporting sentences?

_____ Is your writing easy to read? What changes can you make so it is?

SESSION TWO

Checking for Punctuation and Mechanics

• Read one sentence at a time.

_____ Does every sentence begin with a capital letter?

_____ Does every sentence end with proper punctuation?

_____ Do all your sentences express one clear idea?

SESSION THREE

Checking for Spelling

_____ Circle lightly any words that don't look right.

_____ Use a dictionary to check spelling.

Convince Me!

MATHEMATICS FOCUS

Discussing Strategies

A network of patterns and relationships can be constructed among the basic arithmetic facts. Many problems can be solved with mental arithmetic.

In a whole-class discussion format, students explain their thinking and solutions for addition, subtraction, and multiplication problems solved using mental arithmetic. Students then write in their journals about one other problem.

······································

PREPARATION Familiarize yourself with the Guidelines for "Convince Me!" Discussions and the suggested problems (page 190). Have journals available.

TIME 4 sessions, then ongoing throughout the year

WRITING FOCUS

Keeping a Math Journal

The informal writing students do in journals creates opportunities to find out how students feel about themselves and mathematics, and serves as a tool for reflection and self-assessment.

Students extend their writing about "Convince Me!" problems to include writing about their attitudes and feelings about mathematics. A collection of entries becomes a vehicle for an end of the year reflection by each student.

······································

PREPARATION Provide a journal for each student and for yourself.

TIME 1 session, then on a weekly basis throughout the year

Discussing Strategies

It's amazing how much we can figure out ourselves when we use number sense and our own ability to think to solve problems.

THINKING ON OUR OWN

Problems for "Convince Me!" Discussions

13 + 5	35 × 4	14 × 4
143 + 25	17 − 4	235 − 15
128 + 11	51 − 9	14 + 6
12 × 5	124 − 23	25 × 8
16 × 5	20 × 4	35 − 15

1 For the next several days, familiarize your class with the "Convince Me!" way of thinking about problems. Select problems from the box at left, or others you create, presenting and discussing one at a time. On the chalkboard, write a problem. *Think about the answer to this problem.* Follow the Guidelines for "Convince Me!" Discussions, below.

Guidelines for "Convince Me!" Discussions

- After presenting a problem, allow time for students to think about and solve it. Ask for students' responses. Record the different solutions on the board.

- Do not indicate the rightness or wrongness of each answer. Be aware of any hints your body language or the inflection of your voice might convey.

- Encourage a class debate about the correct solution, requesting that students "convince" each other and you of their thinking.

- Insist that students' explanations rely on number sense, not on following rules.

- Ask for several different explanations for each problem. Does everyone agree? Can someone tell us a different way to think about the problem?

- As students explain their thinking, allow them to discover their own errors. Let the final conclusion about which answer is right come from the class, through discourse, not from you.

WRITING TO CONVINCE

2 At the end of each math time, write on the chalkboard three or four problems similar to those you've been discussing. *In your journal, write one of these problems and its answer. Explain your thinking. Be convincing!*

Keeping a Math Journal

As we write in journals, an extended conversation about our learning becomes part of our experience of mathematics.

WRITING ABOUT THINKING

1 *Your journal will be a diary of your own thinking, a record of your journey in mathematics this year. It will also let me know more about your thinking, and enable me to respond to you individually.*

2 In addition to the "Convince Me!" problems, a question about how students are feeling about their ability to solve problems should be the topic of journal writing once a week or so.

- *What problem were you particularly proud of solving? Tell why.*

- *Have there been problems presented that you have had a difficult time understanding? Explain.*

- *Do you enjoy the "Convince Me!" discussions? Why or why not?*

- *Explain how someone else solved a problem and how you thought about it differently.*

- *Tell about what you are particularly good at in math.*

REVISING TO SHARE

3 Periodically, have students choose one of their journal entries and revise it for someone else to read. *Select an entry that reflects your best thinking or discusses a question that you have.* Refer students to their editing checklists.

4 As students revise their entries, conference with individuals to focus their editing strategies. Suggest one or two proofreading activities.

5 Collect students' revised journal entries and pass them out randomly. *Please read the journal entry and respond.*

TIME FOR REFLECTION

6 Make a note in your plan book to ask students at the end of the year to select ten journal entries that best illustrate the development of their learning of mathematics. Students should give each entry a title, create a table of contents, and write a brief introduction.

ASSESSMENT

Students' self-confidence and disposition toward mathematics influence their success as problem solvers. Use the journals to assess each student's thinking and feelings about mathematics.

- *How does the student view herself as a mathematician?*

- *Is the student able to think about strategies used to solve a problem?*

(Classroom Talk)

ENCOURAGING THE JOURNAL CONVERSATION

Journals are a wonderful vehicle for extended, individual conversations with your students. To encourage journal writing, follow these guidelines.

- Keep your own journal. Occasionally share your journal entries with your students.
- Allow students some privacy in their journals. Have a way students indicate pages they wish you to read. Let students know ahead of time about any entries you plan to read.
- Encourage students to write without concern for mechanics.
- When responding, show your interest by acknowledging students' feelings, praising their thinking or honesty, sharing your own ideas on a subject, or asking questions which prompt students to clarify or extend their thinking.
- Don't keep the students' journals longer than twenty-four hours. Respond in writing to every journal entry you read. Some responses may be very short–simple statements of agreement or short prompts.

Boxes in Boxes

MATHEMATICS FOCUS

Applying Measurement Skills

Between any two whole numbers on a number line, there are fractional numbers that describe various points.

Students explore the fractions represented by the calibration marks on their rulers. They measure a collection of items to the nearest fraction of an inch and compare their determinations.

....

MATERIALS

❑ Vinyl Inch-Metric Ruler (one per student)

❑ overhead ruler

❑ full sheets of paper

PREPARATION   Prepare a paper bag for each group of four students containing an identical collection of 6 or 8 different objects to be measured.

TIME   1 session

WRITING FOCUS

Giving Directions

Written directions for measuring should include a short introduction, an organized list of steps, and words that signal transitions.

Students discuss the difficulties of measuring accurately, then small groups write general directions for measuring. Individuals write directions for measuring one object, then try to follow each other's directions.

....

MATERIALS

❑ chart paper

❑ writing paper

TIME   2 sessions

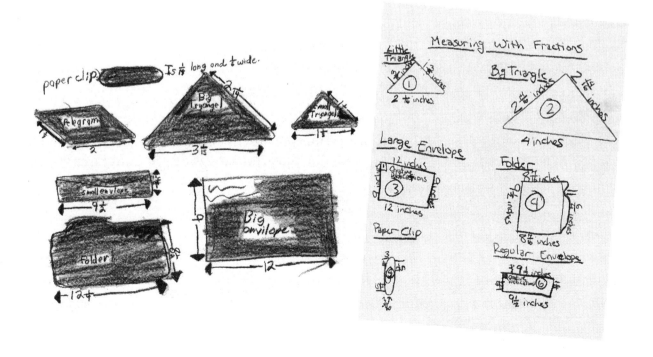

Applying Measurement Skills

We see how our measuring skills measure up. Reading our rulers precisely requires a sharp eye.

READING MARKS FOR FRACTIONAL PARTS

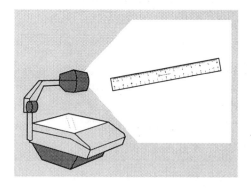

1 Have the students refer to the inch side of their rulers as you display the overhead ruler. ***Look at the segment between zero and one. What do you notice about the marks on the ruler?*** Have the class identify any marks that represent fractional parts of inches, including marks for increments of $\frac{1}{2}$ inch, $\frac{1}{4}$ inch, $\frac{1}{8}$ inches, and $\frac{1}{16}$ inch.

2 Point to various marks on the overhead ruler, as you ask, ***Who can tell me what this measurement would be? What is the most straightforward way of reading that measurement?*** Sometimes, reverse the question, naming a measurement ($2\frac{1}{8}$ inches, for example) and having the students locate that point on their rulers. Ask a volunteer to come up to the overhead projector and show the measurement on the overhead ruler.

MEASURING ITEMS PRECISELY

It's $2\frac{3}{4}$ of an inch. You could say it's $2\frac{6}{8}$, too. That's the same as $2\frac{3}{4}$.

The simplest way is 2 and $\frac{3}{4}$.

3 Distribute to each group of four one of the identical bags of items that you have prepared. Explain that each student should measure and record the length of each item in their group's bag as precisely as they can, using the fraction marks on their rulers. ***Later, you'll be comparing measurements to see how accurate you were.*** As the students work, circulate to make sure individuals know how to read the calibrations on the ruler.

4 Near the end of math time, bring the class together to share findings. For each item measured, use a "Convince Me" discussion format to let the students debate which measurement describes the item most precisely. If there is trouble reaching consensus, put the object in question on the overhead projector alongside the transparent ruler, and have the students read that measurement to compare with their own.

Giving Directions

Describing how to measure accurately is a challenge.

SHARING OUR EXPERIENCES

At first I was measuring from the end of the ruler rather than beginning with the zero.

The difference between one-eighth of an inch and one-sixteenth of an inch is so small that a slight move will make a big difference.

GIVING DIRECTIONS

Transition Words

first   to begin with

second   then   next

finally   last

1 *You've all done a great job measuring. One thing we all learned is that it's not easy to take exact measurements. What are some of the things that kept us from taking exact measurements?* Let students report and exchange ideas.

2 Have groups of four discuss and write up a general list of steps they took to measure any of the items in their bags. Encourage the students to skip a line between each step to make editing their steps easier.

3 When the groups are done writing their steps, have them share their thinking. *Did anyone have additional or different steps?* Encourage the students to get ideas from others to make their own lists more clear and complete.

4 *Now your challenge is to write directions for measuring one of the items in your bag.* Although students may use the notes the group wrote together, they should each write their directions individually. Have students include in their directions a short introduction and an organized list of steps.

5 Encourage the students to use words that signal transitions to help their directions flow clearly from one step to the next. Write the transition words at left on chart paper. During the remainder of the year, the list may be added to as students encounter other transition words and phrases.

REVISING DIRECTIONS

6 After putting their writing away for at least a day, students should return to their directions. *Read your directions. Do only what they say. Are your directions clear?* Allow time for students to revise and edit their writing.

> Throughout *Writing Mathematics*, revising and editing are presented as one step. They do, however, involve two different processes. The focus of revising is the structure and content of the text, whereas the focus of editing is the mechanics. Help students manage this stage of writing by selecting particular revision and editing tasks to address.

STEP BY STEP

7 Collect the students' directions, and randomly pass them out to the students. *Read through the directions step-by-step. Can you follow the directions to complete the task?*

8 Once students have followed the directions, allow time for sharing their results.

ASSESSMENT

To assess this writing activity, evaluate how well the students communicate what they have learned about measurement in their written directions.

- *Did the student write clear, complete steps to describe the process of measuring an object?*

- *Did the student include an introduction and transition words?*

(Classroom Talk)

USING DISCOURSE TO PROMOTE THINKING

Students' thinking is revealed as they verbalize ideas. As students exchange ideas, they begin to engage in processes of metacognition– monitoring, regulating, and evaluating. Participation in groups and in whole class discussions helps students generate new ideas and transfer what is learned to new situations with greater success.

In this lesson, students discuss the problems of taking accurate measurements and their procedures for measuring. The lists of steps for measuring generated by small groups are more clear and complete than would be lists created without discussion by individuals.

Fraction "Do's" and "Don'ts"

MATHEMATICS FOCUS

Formulating Theories

For any given fraction, we can determine other, equivalent fractions. Equivalence thinking is the basis for adding and subtracting fractions.

Students use fraction pieces and common sense to model, solve, and formulate rules for a variety of fraction addition and subtraction problems.

······································

MATERIALS

❏ chart paper

❏ full sheets of paper

    For each pair

❏ Fraction Circles PLUS™

PREPARATION Copy True or False Equations, shown on the opposite page, onto a transparency.

TIME 4 sessions

WRITING FOCUS

Giving Directions

Some components of good directions are: a short introduction, a list of materials, numbered steps, and illustrations. Writing conferences help students revise the directions they write.

Students review commercial directions, then write the directions for solving a fraction problem. After students revise their directions, they have them evaluated by fifth graders.

······································

MATERIALS

❏ writing paper

PREPARATION Collect sample directions from recipes, games, and "how-to" books. Arrange for a fifth-grade class to read your students' directions.

TIME 2-3 sessions

Problem Bank		
Day 1	Day2	Day 3
$\frac{1}{3} + \frac{2}{6}$	$\frac{2}{3} - \frac{1}{2}$	$\frac{1}{2} + \frac{1}{10}$
$\frac{6}{8} - \frac{3}{8}$	$\frac{5}{10} - \frac{1}{2}$	$\frac{3}{4} - \frac{1}{2}$
$\frac{1}{2} + \frac{1}{3}$	$\frac{1}{6} + \frac{2}{3}$	$\frac{1}{10} + \frac{1}{5}$
$\frac{1}{8} + \frac{3}{4}$	$\frac{1}{3} + \frac{1}{4}$	$\frac{3}{4} + \frac{3}{8}$

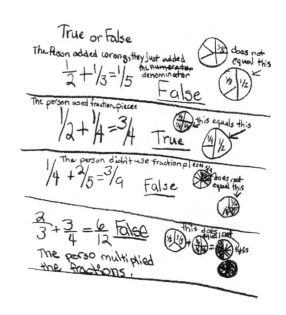

Formulating Theories

Our goal is to make sense of addition and subtraction involving fractions.

1 *You're going to be playing sleuths, figuring out the "do's" and "don'ts" for doing addition and subtraction with fractions.* On the overhead projector, display the list of equations you've prepared. Have pairs use fraction pieces and sketches to model each equation and determine whether it is true or false. *For equations you decide are false, explain the error in thinking someone might have made.*

FORMULATING THE "DON'TS"

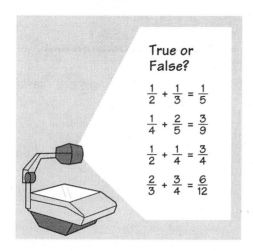

True or False?

$$\frac{1}{2} + \frac{1}{3} = \frac{1}{5}$$

$$\frac{1}{4} + \frac{2}{5} = \frac{3}{9}$$

$$\frac{1}{2} + \frac{1}{4} = \frac{3}{4}$$

$$\frac{2}{3} + \frac{3}{4} = \frac{6}{12}$$

2 At the end of math time, discuss each equation.

- *Did you find a false equation? What error in thinking do you think someone made?*

- *Based on the error, can you come up with a "don't" rule for adding fractions?*

3 Start a list on chart paper, titled "Fraction Addition Don'ts" and add to it the "don't" rules as students suggest them.

4 *Now, I'd like to see if you can figure out the "do's" rules for adding and subtracting fractions.* Ask students to convince you that the equation, 1/2 + 1/4 = 3/4 is true. When they have, note that they thought about 1/2 in a different way in order to add the fractions. *Pay attention to that idea. It's a "do" rule you will find very helpful.*

FORMULATING THE "DO'S"

$\frac{1}{2}$ is the same as $\frac{2}{4}$. So it's the same as adding $\frac{2}{4}$ and $\frac{1}{4}$, and that's $\frac{3}{4}$.

5 Each day, write on the board one list of problems from the Problem Bank on the opposite page. Have pairs use their fraction pieces to solve as many problems as they can. Students should use words, numbers, and sketches to record how they reached a solution for each problem, and keep a list of what they think are the "do's" for addition and subtraction of fractions.

6 End each day with a discussion of students' ideas.

- *How did you figure out one of the problems today?*

- *Who tried a different way?*

- *Who can explain their latest ideas on how to add or subtract fractions?*

Giving Directions

We really have to think about what we know when we try to explain adding or subtracting fractions to another student.

THINKING ABOUT DIRECTIONS

1 *Over the last few days you have solved many fraction addition and subtraction problems. Now your challenge will be to write directions for adding and subtracting fractions.*

2 *First, let's think about what good directions include.* Have pairs review the commercial directions you have provided and identify their components. Bring the class together to discuss the components, including title, introduction, list of materials, numbered steps, and illustrations. Discuss what makes directions easy or difficult to follow.

3 Write five or six fraction addition problems on the board. Challenge students to choose a problem and write directions for solving it. *Work through the problem thinking about what you do to solve it. Make notes to yourself about the steps you take.*

WRITING DIRECTIONS

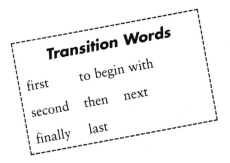

Transition Words

first   to begin with

second   then   next

finally   last

4 Have students use their notes to write directions that a fifth-grade student could follow to solve the problem. Their directions should include a title, short introduction, step-by-step directions, and a materials list and illustrations if needed.

> It may be helpful to have a class discussion about the audience, fifth graders. Encourage students to think about what a fifth-grade student knows and ways they can make their directions clear to that audience.

5 Write the words shown at left on chart paper. Explain that these words signal transitions. Encourage students to use them to help their directions flow clearly from one step to the next. Add to the list during the year as students encounter other transitional words and phrases.

EDITING PROCEDURES

6 Have students trade papers. They should follow the directions they received, then write one good thing about them and one or more suggestions for improvement. When the writers receive the suggestions, provide time for students to revise their directions.

ONE STEP AT A TIME

7 Give the students' directions to a fifth-grade class. Have the teacher explain to her students that they should follow the directions exactly, not use their own methods. The students should record how they followed the directions for solving the problem and write about how easy or difficult the directions were to follow.

8 When the responses are returned, provide time for your students to discuss them. You may want to provide time for revising directions and trying again.

- *Was the student able to follow your directions?*

- *Were there things you could have done to make your directions more clear?*

ASSESSMENT

To assess this writing activity, evaluate how well students communicate their understanding of fractions in directions for fifth graders.

- *Did the student use fraction equivalencies and rules for solving fraction problems?*

- *Did the student incorporate the components of good directions?*

-------------------------------(Classroom Talk)-------------------------------

ENCOURAGING THE EXCHANGE OF IDEAS

Classroom discussions in which students have opportunities to share their ideas and listen to the views of their peers make students active participants in their own learning and promote real understandings of mathematics. As part of the discourse in your classroom, expect students to pose questions and to probe, challenge, and elaborate upon the ideas exchanged.

In many classrooms, students have come to rely on the teacher as the sole judge of "right" and "wrong." Consequently, many students hold back responses unless they are reasonably sure they have the right answer, and then look to the teacher for validation. By directing students to their peers for validation or for other viewpoints, you will change the old communication pattern.

PART VI

Linking Math and Technology

teddy and Me
MEASURING AND COMPARING LENGTH

WHAT IS THIS INVESTIGATION ABOUT?

We go to great lengths to measure our own stuffed animals that we bring from home. We use LinkerCube units, and *How many?* is the question we ask as we measure hands, legs, paws, tummies, height, smiles, arms, and more. This language we use to make these comparisons carries over into our computer project.

PLANNING FOR THE INVESTIGATION...

Manipulatives Kit	*For each pair:* 100 LinkerCubes® in one color
Paper	12" x 18" drawing paper (or larger to trace outline of large stuffed animals)
Software	*The Graph Club*
Preparation	Each child should bring a stuffed animal from home. (It's a good idea to have a few "extras" on hand.)

before the investigation...

Gather the children and their stuffed animals on the rug. Have them introduce their animals. **Let's do some comparing.** Call on a child to put his animal in the center. **Do any of you think your animal is taller than this?** Make several comparisons with the animals, using language such as *bigger* or *smaller*, *lighter* or *darker*, *more* or *less*, and so on.

INITIATING THE INVESTIGATION...

1. *First, we'll make pictures of our animals.* Show the children how to trace outlines of their animals on paper. Then they can color them to make life-sized portraits.

2. *We're going to measure our animals with LinkerCubes. How many cubes do you think it would take to go from the tip of your rabbit's tail to his neck?* Show how to place the cubes directly on the outline. Have the child write the numbers of the length on the outline.

3. *What are some things we might want to measure?* Have the children suggest different parts to measure (from ear to ear, leg, foot, height). Write the suggestions on the chalkboard with words and rebuses. The children should measure the parts of their animals in cubes and record the measurements on their animal pictures.

> This would be a good time to pay attention to the kinds of words you and the children are using to describe the different measurements. Their language will be imprecise at first, as they confuse taller and bigger, for example, but will improve during the investigation.

13 cubes

INTEGRATING SOFTWARE INTO THE INVESTIGATION...

We get to know our animals ever better when we enter their vital statistics onto the computer. It's easier to compare noses when we use state-of-the-art graphs!

Open *The Graph Club*
Select Create
Select Graph
Choose how many to graph
Type in your title

1 ▌ ***Let's try making a graph that compares the measurements of our animals.*** Have the children bring their recordings to the computer. Show them how to set the table up for the number of body parts they've measured. Show them that the measurements in The Graph Club only go up to 10, so they can only graph measurements that are 10 or less. **What title could we use?** Type in the title the children suggest.

Select Choose Symbols
Drag the symbols into the bins
Click OK
Select Make Another Graph
Label the symbols

2 ***Can anyone find the LinkerCubes to show our measurement numbers?*** Select LinkerCubes as the symbol for each bin. Call on a volunteer to drag the LinkerCube from the middle window and drop it on top of the symbol they wish to replace. Repeat this for the remainder of the symbols. Choose Make Another Graph and label the LinkerCubes with the body parts that were measured.

Tedy Ber	
What?	How Many?
arm	4
leg	3
foot	3
hed	5

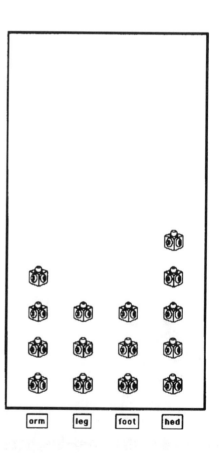

Type in your data
Choose Make Another Graph

Select File
Select Print Graphs
Choose which graphs to print
Drag your graphs to rearrange them
Click OK
Select Print

3 ***Now we can enter our measurements.*** Have volunteers come up and enter the number of cubes in the appropriate spot. After the data has been entered, let volunteers click the Graph Type buttons at the bottom of the screen to view the data in different forms. Discuss with the children why table and bar graphs work better for measurement.

4 Print the graphs. Encourage the children to admire their measurement recordings and the graphs made on the computer. Invite the children to take time to do some comparing.

- ***Can you compare two measurements on your recording? on your graph?***
- ***Which animal was the tallest? The shortest?***

Was it easier to compare the measurements you made on your recording or on the computer graph?

" The tracing because you could just look at the number written. On the graph you had to count the LinkerCubes. **"**

" I think the computer graph because you don't have to count the cubes, just look at which one is taller. **"**

How about someone else?

Surveys

EXPLORING WAYS TO REPORT DATA

WHAT IS THIS INVESTIGATION ABOUT?

We explore data by pursuing our own interests. We focus on a very important theme in mathematics—using writing to communicate to others what we find out. The tools we use for communication go beyond paper and pencil to the computer. We're challenged, but in a most enjoyable way, because we're getting to know each other in the process.

PLANNING FOR THE INVESTIGATION...

Paper	full sheets of paper, eighth sheets of paper, 2-cm grid paper (page 210) cut into strips, 12" × 18" drawing paper
Supplies	scissors, paste
Software	*The Graph Club*
Preparation	Take three legal-size envelopes and tape each one to an $8\frac{1}{2}$" × 11" sheet of paper.

before the investigation...

To practice organizing data, have students print their first name on grid paper strips, one letter in each box. Have them count the letters. Ask questions to prompt their thinking: **How many letters does the longest name have? How many start with a bumpy letter? a straight letter?** Have the class choose a favorite way of organizing the names and hang them up on the wall.

HOW LONG IS YOUR NAME?

3 letters	4 letters	5 letters
Amy	Luis	Danny
	Erin	Kevin
		Laura
		Kalil

6 letters	7 letters	8 letters
Jeremy	Kasinda	Jullianna
Marisa	Michael	
mikika	Awenira	
Robbie		

INITIATING THE INVESTIGATION...

We take surveys and communicate our personal data on posters. That's *one* way to show it...

▶ Resist the temptation to "help" the children by organizing their work for them. Instead of hurrying to suggest conventional ways of ordering the information, let the children communicate to you what they see as important. Ask open-ended questions, and listen. This prepares the children for organizing the data in their own ways.

1 **Let's brainstorm a list of questions you'd like to ask your classmates.** On the chalkboard, write the questions as the children name them. Tell the children to choose questions that will have 10 or fewer responses, since that is the limit of what *The Graph Club* can show.

2 **Let's find out the answers to these questions for the whole class.** Write each question on a piece of paper to which an envelope has been attached. Pin these papers up where everyone can see them.

3 **Write your name and the answer to each of the three questions on your strip of paper. Use numbers, words, and pictures to answer the different questions.** Tell the children to put each answer paper in the envelope for that question.

4 Arrange the children's answers on sheets of paper and make multiple copies of each sheet. Let partners choose answer sheets for the questions they want to answer. **Work with your partner to make a poster.** Have pairs cut out and organize the answers on drawing paper. **Write a sentence or two about what you found out.**

INTEGRATING SOFTWARE INTO THE INVESTIGATION...

Another way to show our data is to graph what we've learned on the computer. Now we know a lot about each other and we can show it in many ways.

Open *The Graph Club*
Select Create
Type in your title

1 As pairs finish their posters, have them bring their work to the computer. ***Let's show your findings on a graph. We'll type in a title. Who can think of one?*** Let one child type in the title.

Select Graph
Choose how many to graph

2 ***What are the answers you got on your survey?*** Help the pair set up *The Graph Club* for the same number of elements in the graph as the number of answers they have named.

Select Choose Symbols
Drag the symbols into the bins
Click OK

3 ***What symbols can you find to show your data?*** Many sets of symbols in *The Graph Club* are appropriate for class surveys: ice cream flavors, cartoon characters, fruits, and so on. Show the children how to drag the desired symbol from the middle window and place it over the symbol they wish to replace. Repeat this for the remainder of the symbols. If a symbol they need is not in *The Graph Club*, let pairs brainstorm a way to handle this.

Title	
What?	**How Many?**
🍎	8
🍓	6
🍐	5
🍇	9
🍎	4

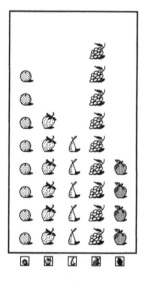

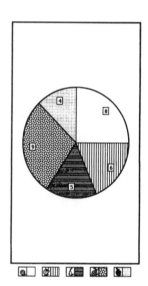

Type in your data
Select Make Another Graph
Choose a graph type
Save Your Graph

Select File
Select Print Graphs
Choose which graphs to print
Drag your graphs to rearrange
  them
Click OK
Select Print

THINKING ABOUT THE INVESTIGATION...

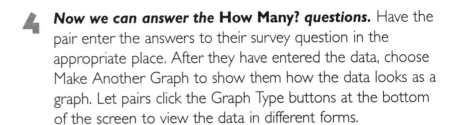

4 ***Now we can answer the How Many? questions.*** Have the pair enter the answers to their survey question in the appropriate place. After they have entered the data, choose Make Another Graph to show them how the data looks as a graph. Let pairs click the Graph Type buttons at the bottom of the screen to view the data in different forms.

5 When pairs find one or more kinds of graphs that explain their data, they can print them out. Some may enjoy coloring them as a final step.

At the end of the investigation, have the children bring their posters and graphs to the rug. Take time to talk about each one.

- ***Show us your poster and tell us what you found out. How does your graph tell what you found out?***
- ***In what ways is the graph different from the poster? How is it the same?***

Tell us about your question.

" Our question was 'What kind of pet do you have?' and we found out that most people have cats. **"**

How did you decide how to organize your poster?

" We made groups for the different pets and we put them in rows. All the cats are in a row and all the dogs are in a different row. People who didn't have any pets got a zero. **"**

How does your graph show this?

" For the zero, there's just no picture. **"**

2-CM GRID

To the Teacher: Permission is given to reproduce this page.

thousands collections

COLLECTING AND DISPLAYING ONE THOUSAND ITEMS

WHAT IS THIS INVESTIGATION ABOUT?

What does one thousand of something look like? We collect 1000 items and find that the way they look can differ greatly, depending on what the 1000 items are! We find creative ways to count efficiently, keep track of what we have already counted, and display our Thousands Collections so that we can see, without having to count each item, that there are 1000. Our computer presentations add a lot to our understanding of big numbers.

PLANNING FOR THE INVESTIGATION...

Paper	full sheets of paper, chart paper
Software	*The Multimedia Workshop*
Preparation	Have general supplies available that the students might need for counting and for creating their displays, such as tape, cups, or large pieces of butcher paper.

before the investigation...

Have a brainstorming session on ideas for Thousands Collections. As the students suggest items to collect and organize, record their ideas on chart paper.

Ideas for
Thousands Collections

draw stars

beans

buttons

spiders

baseball cards

LinkerCube rows

INITIATING THE INVESTIGATION...

We make collections of 1000 items. It seems like an impossibly huge task till we have a plan. Then the challenge is how to keep track of it all!

> Some groups may choose a collection that you doubt they will be able to complete. Don't worry or intervene with their plans. Let them know that revising their plan is part of understanding what 1000 really is.

1 *Each group of four will collect or make 1000 things and then make a display that proves you have 1000. Let's look at our list of suggestions for our Thousand Collections.* Have the groups choose an idea from the list or another idea they agree on.

2 *What are some ways you might show your collection?* Tell them to make a plan that tells how they will collect and display the 1000 things. *Have someone in your group write about how you will collect and display your items. Also make a list of materials you will need to make your display, such as tape, cups, or large pieces of butcher paper.*

> Encourage the students to use various counting strategies. Some will adopt counting strategies that involve groups, such as putting items into groups of ten and then counting by tens. As these strategies are shared, other students will have the opportunity to consider them.

3 Give the group some time to collect, count, and record their collections. As they work, visit with the groups individually and discuss what they're doing. *How many items do you have for your collection so far? How are you keeping track of the number of items? How much space do you think your collection will need?* (Imagine a collection of 1000 inflated balloons!)

4 As the students finish their Thousands Collections displays, take a tour of the classroom and discuss the ways different groups solved difficulties that came up as they worked.

This is 100

There are 10 100's in this bag = 1000!

INTEGRATING SOFTWARE INTO THE INVESTIGATION...

We find even more moving ways to show 1000. Some of us are content with picture proof, but others produce a movie—sound and all—to show what they've done.

1 Have the groups brainstorm about ways to show 1000 on the computer. *What computer tools could you use to show so many items? Talk to your group about how you want your pictures or movie to look. Use notes and sketches to remind you of ways to organize your Thousand Collection on the computer.*

Open *The Multimedia Workshop*
Select Paint Workshop
Create your illustration
Save **your illustration**
Open Libraries
Import **clip art**
Save **your illustration**

2 Some students may want to work only in the **Paint Workshop** to create one or several images (either their own creations, clip art, or photographs) to show their Thousands Collections.

Select Video Workshop Scene
  Maker
Import **your illustration**
Select a background
Type in your text
Save **your scene**
Select Video Workshop Sequencer
Import **your scene**
Select a transition
Place your transition
Save **your movie**

3 Other students may feel comfortable making several scenes in the **Video Workshop Scene Maker** and then using the **Sequencer** to animate their scenes. The most sophisticated users could add transitions and sounds and music for a very elaborate presentation.

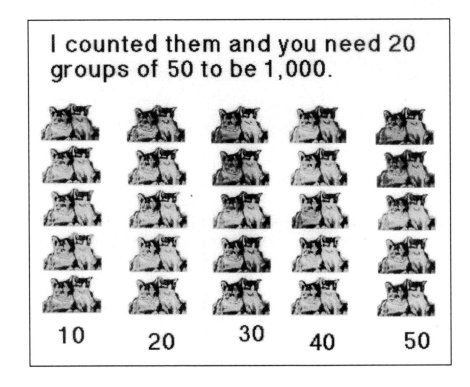

I counted them and you need 20 groups of 50 to be 1,000.

10   20   30   40   50

Select Writing Workshop
Select Print

Open Playback
Click Save & Play
Select Auto Play

THINKING ABOUT THE INVESTIGATION...

4 Students who created only an illustration may want to write about their collection and then print their Thousands Collections illustrations at the end of the investigation.

5 If some students have made movies, choose a time when the entire class can watch their presentations. *Let's watch these movies to see other ways to understand 1000.*

Toward the end of the investigation, review the presentations. Talk with the students about their work and what they learned.

- *What new things did you learn about big numbers?*
- *How can you tell there are 1000 items here without counting them?*

What was the hardest part of the investigation?

" *Keeping track of the buttons. We forgot which ones we counted. Then we put them in cups so we only had to count by hundreds.* "

" *Remembering how many Cut and Pastes we should do.* "

" *We made a movie. It went too fast so it was hard to count the thousand.* "

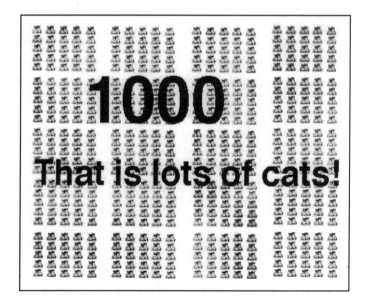

valentine patterns

CREATING, EXTENDING, AND PREDICTING PATTERNS

WHAT IS THIS INVESTIGATION ABOUT?

We examine and extend patterns to define the rules that govern them. We figure out the rules and discover that we can make accurate predictions based on our rules. Then we use the computer to help us visualize patterns and compute formulas. When we input the formulas, we are actually telling the rule!

PLANNING FOR THE INVESTIGATION...

Paper	full sheets of paper, quarter sheets of paper, chart paper
Supplies	calculators
Software	*The Cruncher*

before the investigation...

Give students some practice with patterns and rules by asking them to solve this problem. **Let's pretend we're farmers who have a herd of cows. Our cows need to be fenced in. To build a fence around 1 cow, it takes 8 cubes. To build a fence around 2 cows, it takes 10 cubes. To build a fence around 3 cows, it takes 12 cubes. How many cubes does it take to build a fence around 10 cows?**

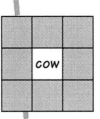

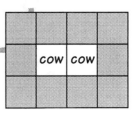

INITIATING THE INVESTIGATION...

Off we go to solve a problem about valentines. We see a pattern and we make a rule that explains it.

1 **Let's begin by acting out a valentine problem.** Have each student draw a heart on a quarter sheet of paper to use as a valentine. As you explain the problem, ask students to act it out by delivering their valentines. Begin to create a chart of the numbers.

2 **The first time the door bell rings, there is 1 person at the door with a valentine. The total number of valentines delivered is 1.** Have a student put these numbers on the chart. **The second time the doorbell rings, 3 people bring valentines. Now the total number of valentines that have been delivered is 4.** Have another student add these numbers to the chart.

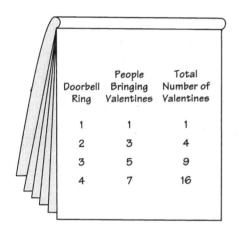

Doorbell Ring	People Bringing Valentines	Total Number of Valentines
1	1	1
2	3	4
3	5	9
4	7	16

3 Continue to have students act out the problem. With each ring of the doorbell, tell the class how many people should arrive with valentines. (Each time, 2 more people bring valentines than the number that brought them the last time.) Point to the People Bringing Valentines column. **How are the numbers in this column changing?**

▶ The total number of valentines delivered is the number of doorbell rings, squared. For 10 rings there will be 10 x 10 valentines, or 100.

4 **After the doorbell has rung 10 times, what do you think the total number of valentines will be?** Write the students' predictions on the chalkboard to discuss at the end of the investigation. **With your partner, figure out how many valentines there will be after 10 rings of the doorbell and make a chart that shows your thinking.**

INTEGRATING SOFTWARE INTO THE INVESTIGATION...

With our charts in hand, we're ready to create our own spreadsheets. It's amazing how fast the computer "learns" our rules!

1 Have pairs bring their charts to the computer. **Let's use a spreadsheet to show what we know.** Review the elements in a spreadsheet: *formula bar, rows, columns,* and *cells.* **We'll do one together, then you and your partner can make your own spreadsheet.**

Open *The Cruncher*
Select New Spreadsheet
Select a cell
Type your title in the cell
Select Save

2 **We'll start with a blank spreadsheet. What do you think would be a good title to enter into a cell?** Type in Valentine Patterns. **What column headings could we enter in our spreadsheet?** Have a volunteer type in appropriate column headings.

Select a cell
Type your data in the cell
Click on the check
Select Save

3 **What data would you put in the first column?** Have students come up and enter the numbers up to the fourth ring in the appropriate cells.

Select a cell
Type an equal sign
Type in your formula
Click on the check
Select Save

4 **How could we get the computer to compute the answers for us? What formula could you use to get the right numbers in the column titled Number of People?** (the number in the cell above it +2) Remind students that they must use an equal sign to make a formula. Go back and forth between the data and the solutions until students are comfortable with the formula. Continue this for all four rows. **What about the formula for Total Valentines?** (the number of the cell times itself: =A5*A5) Show this procedure for only the first cell in this column.

	A	B	C	D	E	F
1	*Valentine Patterns*					
2						
3	*Doorbell Ring*		*People Bringing Valentines*		*Total Number of Valentines*	
4						
5	1		1		=A5*A5	
6	2		=C5+2		=A6*A6	
7	3		=C6+2		=A7*A7	
8	4		=C7+2		=A8*A8	
9	5		=C8+2		=A9*A9	
10	6		=C9+2		=A10*A10	
11	7		=C10+2		=A11*A11	
12	8		=C11+2		=A12*A12	
13	9		=C12+2		=A13*A13	
14	10		=C13+2		=A14*A14	
15						

5 *What could you say about patterns and rules in the Notes? Use stickers to decorate your spreadsheet and notebook.* Ask a volunteer to type in some words to demonstrate the features of the notebook. Have another demonstrate how to select a sticker and move it around on the spreadsheet or note.

6 Have pairs work at the computer to make a spreadsheet like the one the class did together. Give students time to explore the software options. Encourage them to experiment with the formulas. *Remember to print your spreadsheet and notes.*

THINKING ABOUT THE INVESTIGATION...

Toward the end of the investigation, bring the class together to share and discuss solutions. Have the students bring their charts, spreadsheets, and notes with them.

- *What number did you come up with for the total? How did you figure it out?*
- *What patterns did you notice? How would you describe the rules for this problem?*
- *Now that you know how to figure out 10 rings, what about 12 rings? 15 rings? What would you do to figure out any number of rings?*

Tell us about your spreadsheet.

" *Once we got the formulas in it was really neat. The computer figured out the answers for us.* "

How do you think it did that?

" *Well, look at what's in cell E6. It is =A6*A6. That means that you multiply the number in cell A6 by itself. So that's 2 times 2 which is 4.* "

Did anyone else use a different formula?

ANCieNT AlgoRitHMS
INVESTIGATING ALTERNATIVE METHODS OF MULTIPLICATION

WHAT IS THIS INVESTIGATION ABOUT?

We explore ancient multiplication algorithms that show us that there has always been more than one way to get the correct answer. Our mathematical power and technical acuity is increased as we choose one of these algorithms to present as a video.

PLANNING FOR THE INVESTIGATION...

Manipulatives Kit *For each pair:*
Base Ten Blocks (2 hundreds, 10 tens, 20 ones)

Paper full sheets of paper

Supplies calculators

Software *The Multimedia Workshop*

Preparation Make one copy of the Russian Peasant Multiplication algorithm, the Egyptian Multiplication algorithm, and Lattice Multiplication algorithm (pages 223–224) for each pair.

before the iNVestigAtioN...

Introduce Base Ten Blocks as one strategy for solving two-digit multiplication problems. On the board, write the equation 3 × 4 = 12. **Three rows of 4 equals 12.** Encourage groups of four to use Base Ten Blocks to build a rectangle with 3 rows of 4 blocks. Draw the solution on the board. Continue this with more challenging problems: 10 × 10, 12 × 13, and so on, using the "rows of" language.

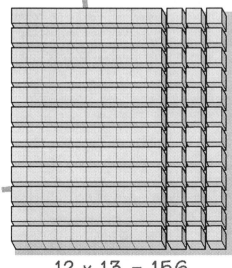

12 × 13 = 156

INITIATING THE INVESTIGATION...

Investigating ancient algorithms is fun and challenging! They even make us think about some of the strategies we use...

> In Egypt, the basic arithmetic operation was addition—our operation of multiplication was first performed through successive doubling. India seems to be where lattice multiplication began; it was carried to China and Arabia. Used in Italy by the fourteenth and fifteenth centuries, it was called *gelosia* because it resembled the window gratings in Venice.

> Presenting these different problem-solving strategies—manipulatives, algorithms, and calculators—further reinforces the idea that there are many ways to solve an arithmetic problem. When solving problems, it is important for students to find strategies that make sense to them, rather than merely memorizing one way to do it.

1 *Since the beginning of time, people have been trying to invent quick ways (or short cuts) of figuring out arithmetic problems.* Hand out the sheets on Russian, Egyptian, and lattice multiplication. You may want to discuss the historical significance of these algorithms with the class. Some students may be interested in researching this on their own.

2 As students work with their partners and investigate these ancient algorithms, have them try the same multiplication problems using the Base Ten Blocks. Remind them to use the "rows of" language. Provide calculators for students to check their work.

3 After the students have worked through the algorithms, bring the class together for a discussion. *What problems did you solve using these algorithms? Did you get the correct answer? How do you know? Which of these methods of multiplying was the most efficient? Tell why you think so.*

4 *Decide which ancient algorithm you prefer.* Have students work with their partner and choose together which algorithm they will be making into a video.

INTEGRATING SOFTWARE INTO THE INVESTIGATION...

From the ancient world to the high-tech world—what a leap, but we're up for the challenge!

Open *The Multimedia Workshop*
Select Video Workshop Scene Maker
Open Libraries
Choose Clip Art **or** Photographs
Import **your illustration**
Select a background
Type in your text
Save **your scene**

Select Paint Workshop
Create your illustration
Save **your illustration**
Select Video Workshop Scene
    Maker
Import **your illustration**
Save **your scene**

Select Video Workshop Sequencer
Click on the first box on the
    video track
Import **your scene**
Select a transition
Place your transition
Save **your movie**

1 ***Let's make a video presentation of the algorithm you chose. Start by making a scene—all videos are just a series of scenes.*** Some students may want to begin with illustrations from the Libraries.

2 Other students may prefer to create their own illustrations in the Paint Workshop. ***Let's show how we could solve this algorithm in another scene.*** Remind students of the variety of tools and features available to explain their thinking. Tell the students they can make as many scenes as they want to describe how they solved the problem using the algorithm.

3 After the students have made several scenes, they're ready to make a movie. ***You can put all your scenes together to make a presentation.*** Have students demonstrate for the class how to place several scenes and transitions to remind others of the various steps.

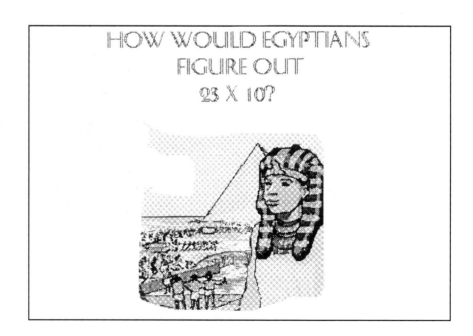

HOW WOULD EGYPTIANS
FIGURE OUT
23 X 10?

Click on the soundtrack
Open Libraries
Open Sound
Select some sound or music
Save **your movie**

Open Playback
Click Save & Play
Select Auto Play

THINKING ABOUT THE INVESTIGATION...

4 **How could words or sound and music add to your presentation?** Students can narrate their movie, or they may choose music or sound from the Libraries.

5 **Now we are ready to watch our creations!** As the pairs finish their investigations, set aside some time for them to give their video presentations to the class.

After all the presentations have been viewed, gather the class together so they can discuss their findings.

- **How did you organize your presentation?**
- **How did you show the algorithm on your presentation?**

How would you show how to use Base Ten Blocks to solve multiplication problems?

" *I would draw the rows of ones and the squares of hundreds.* "

" *And I would make trades and explain it by narrating it on the microphone.* "

Did anyone narrate their ancient algorithm presentation?

 Egyptian Multiplication is really adding.

These are the steps to multiply 23 x 10.

Write	Say
23	Thats 1 of it
23+23=46	Thats 2 of it
46+46=92	Thats 4 of it
92+92=184	Thats 8 of it
184+184=368	Thats 16 of it

 So you keep going down adding the number above on the left and squaring the number in the right column till you stop because the number in the right column is greater than the second number you multiply.

Here stop at 16 of it on the right because thats bigger than 10.
Then which numbers add up to 10? 8+2
Find the numbers that match on the left column. 46+ 184
46 + 184 add up to 230. That's the answer!

Multiply it our way to see!

RUSSIAN PEASANT MULTIPLICATION
21 x 19

1. Make two columns on your paper. Label the first column "Halving" and the second column "Doubling." Write the first number under "Halving" and the second number under "Doubling."

2. Halve the first number until you reach 1, writing the answer each time in the first column. Disregard and remainders.

3. Double the second number, writing the answer each time in the second column. Do this the same number of times it took you to halve the first number.

4. Draw a line through each row that has an even number in the "Halving" column.

5. Add the numbers in the "Doubling" column that do not have a line drawn through them as in the example below:

Halving	Doubling	
21	x	19
~~10~~		~~38~~ ("Halving" number is even.)
5		76
~~2~~		~~152~~ ("Halving" number is even.)
1		304

Add: 19 + 76 + 304 = 399

21 x 19 = 399

LATTICE MULTIPLICATION
455 x 34

- Draw a rectangle with ¢55 across the top and 3¢ down the right side.

- Draw diagonal lines from the upper right to the lower left. Write in the multiplication facts.

- Figure out the sum of the diagonals, starting at the far right.

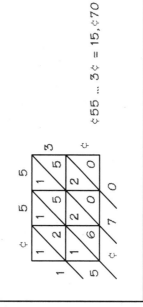

¢55 ... 3¢ = 15, ¢70

EGYPTIAN MULTIPLICATION
69 x 19

1. Write the first number you are multiplying in the first column. Say to yourself, "That's 1 of it." Write this in the second column.

2. Add the first number to itself and write the equation in the first column. Say to yourself, "That's 2 of them." Write this in the second column.

3. Add the sum to itself and write the equation in the first column. Say to yourself, "That's 4 of them." Write this in the second column.

4. Add the sum to itself and write the equation in the first column. Say to yourself, "That's 8 of them." Write this in the second column.

5. Continue this pattern (1, 2, 4, 8, 16, 32, 64, 128, ...) until you say to yourself a number that is greater than the second number you are multiplying. In the example, this number is 32 because 32 is greater than 19.

69	That's 1 of it.
69 + 69 = 138	That's 2 of them.
138 + 138 = 276	That's 4 of them.
276 + 276 = 552	That's 8 of them.
552 + 552 = 1104	That's 16 of them.
1104 + 1104 = 2208	That's 32 of them.

6. Now, find a way to add the numbers you've been writing in the second column so that the sum is exactly the second number you are multiplying, which in this example is 19.

$$16 + 2 + 1 = 19$$

7. Find the corresponding sums in the first column and add them together.

$$1104 + 138 + 69 = 1311$$

$$69 \times 19 = 1311$$

city schools graphs
ANALYZING WAYS TO REPRESENT SETS OF DATA

WHAT IS THIS INVESTIGATION ABOUT?

The superintendent of schools asks our assistance for a presentation he'll make. We look at the data, decide which type of graph will best represent it, and make bar and circle graphs on the computer. Thanks to us, the superintendent's presentation will be technically up-to-date!

PLANNING FOR THE INVESTIGATION...

Manipulatives Kit	*For each pair:* Fraction Circles PLUS™, 100 Rainbow Cubes (33 each of three colors)
Paper	full sheets of paper
Software	*The Cruncher*
Preparation	Make copies of the New Providence Schools Data (page 229) and Urgent Fax! (page 230) for each pair.

before the investigation...

Let's say that our class has been turned into a consulting firm for the fictional city of New Providence. Read this letter to the class.

> School District of New Providence
>
> Dear Class,
>
> I must make a presentation to the school board next week, and the mayor has convinced me that your firm can help. Please organize the raw data I've enclosed into a variety of graphs—some bar graphs and some circle graphs. I look forward to seeing what you come up with.
>
> Sincerely,
>
> *Harold Washington*
>
> Harold Washington
> Superintendent of Schools

INITIATING THE INVESTIGATION...

Our consulting firm rises to the challenge that the superintendent has presented to us.

1 *Here is the data the superintendent sent.* Give each pair a copy of the New Providence Schools Data. Review what the students know about circle graphs. *What do they look like? When have we used them? Talk to your partner and draw a sketch that shows what part of the total number of schools in 1915 were elementary schools.* Have one pair sketch their idea on the chalkboard. Discuss how it should be labeled.

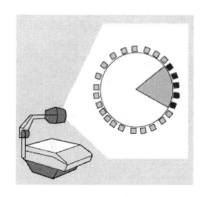

2 *How could we use Fraction Circles to model the same graph? Let's try arranging the Rainbow Cubes representing the fractional part all the way around the whole Fraction Circle piece.* Show this on the overhead projector. *Does this give you any ideas about using your Fraction Circles to model the circle graph?* If no one suggests it, place a one-fifth piece on the whole near the 5 cubes representing the other schools.

3 *The superintendent has sent us an urgent fax.* Hand out the Urgent Fax! Have the students draw circle graphs for question 4 on the fax. *Use your Rainbow Cubes and Fraction Circles to show what fraction of the total elementary and secondary schools each represents. Then draw a circle graph. Remember to title the graph and label each part.* Have two volunteers draw their graphs on the chalkboard and discuss them.

4 *Now think about how to display this data in a bar graph.* Review bar graphs if necessary. *What kinds of data is best shown by a bar graph? a circle graph? Answer the questions from the fax. Include some of each type of graph, and remember to put titles and labels on your graphs.*

▶ Pairs trying to represent similar data for 1975, for example, will not have 90 cubes to show the total. One solution is to let each cube stand for more than one school. The data for 1975 could be roughly shown with 20 cubes of one color, 10 cubes of a second color, and 1 cube of a third color. The parts of the circle could be sectioned off to create the circle graph.

INTEGRATING SOFTWARE INTO THE INVESTIGATION...

We make circle and bar graphs on *The Cruncher* that look so professional we know we're in business!

Open *The Cruncher*
Select New Spreadsheet
Select a cell
Type your title in the cell
Click on the check
Select Save

Select a cell
Type your data in the cell
Click on the check
Select Save

Select a cell
Type your data in the cell
Click on the check
Select Save

Select the cells for the chart
Select Options
Select Chart
Click on the type of chart
Type in a title
Label the x **and** y **axes**
Click OK

1. *Choose a question from the superintendent's fax. You'll answer the superintendent's question using spreadsheets and graphs created on the computer.* Remind students of the parts of a spreadsheet: *row, column, cell,* and *formula bar.* **Let's enter a title for question 2 in a cell.**

2. *Now we'll enter the data from the Number of Schools in New Providence chart.* Have a student enter some data in a cell, such as number of elementary schools in 1975.

3. Continue to have students add data to the cells to answer the question.

4. *Now we'll use our spreadsheet to make circle or bar graphs that answer our question. Who has an idea of how we could do this?* Have the students explore the graphs and decide which show the data best.

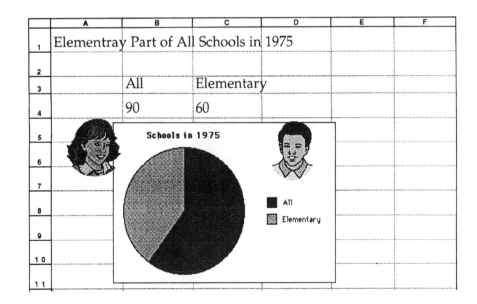

Click Notes
Type in your notes
Select Option
Select Sticker Picker
Choose a sticker
Click OK
Move your sticker

Select File
Select Print

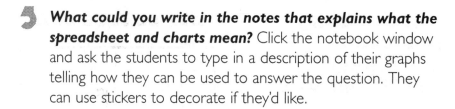

5 *What could you write in the notes that explains what the spreadsheet and charts mean?* Click the notebook window and ask the students to type in a description of their graphs telling how they can be used to answer the question. They can use stickers to decorate if they'd like.

6 *I'd like you and your partner to choose another question to answer and make your own spreadsheet. Then print your spreadsheet and graphs. Color them for the superintendent's presentation.*

THINKING ABOUT THE INVESTIGATION...

Toward the end of the investigation, discuss the graphs made in response to the superintendent's questions.

- *How are circle graphs and bar graphs the same? How are they different?*
- *What can you tell from the graphs you made? What can't you tell?*

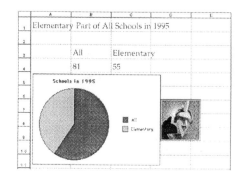

How were the graphs you made useful to the superintendent?

" *Ours would be really useful to him. We compared the number of elementary schools with all the schools from different years.*"

" *Even though the number of schools was different, the portion of the circle graph looked almost the same.*"

" *That showed that there were less elementary schools and less total schools.*"

Those are marvelous comments. Are there any others?

CITY SCHOOL DATA

Number of Schools in New Providence	1875	1895	1915	1935	1955	1975	1995
Elementary Schools	2	4	20	16	32	60	55
Secondary Schools	1	1	4	3	15	29	25
Colleges	1	1	1	1	1	1	1
Total Number of Schools	4	6	25	20	48	90	81

To the Teacher: Permission is given to reproduce this page.

Urgent Fax!

From: Harold J. Washington, Superintendent of Schools

Message: Please use your graphs to answer these questions:

1. How has the overall number of elementary schools changed since 1875?

2. How does the number of elementary schools compare with the total number of schools in 1975? in 1995?

3. What was the ratio of elementary school students to secondary schools students in 1955? in 1995?

4. What was the ratio of elementary schools to secondary schools in 1875? in 1895?

5. How has the overall number of secondary schools changed since 1875?

6. What was the ratio of elementary schools to secondary schools in 1915? in 1935?

7. How does the number of secondary schools compare with the total number of schools in 1975? in 1995?

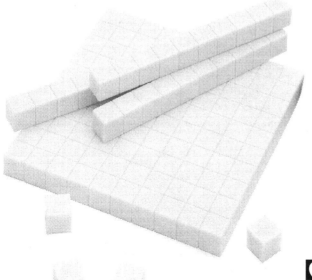

Call now for your
Creative Publications catalog.
With your first order,
we'll send you a set of
100 Thin Pattern Blocks and
Take Off! With Pattern Blocks,
an easy-to-use booklet to
help you get started.

free gift

just for
new teachers.

Simply attach this page
(you may photocopy)
to your order, or refer to
#A025 when ordering
by phone.

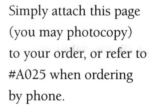

**Welcome to
the Creative
Publications
family!**

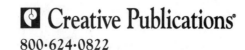